Faculty and Teacher Bargaining

Faculty and Teacher Bargaining

The Impact of Unions on Education

Edited by
George W. Angell
National Academy of Education

LexingtonBooks
D.C. Heath and Company
Lexington, Massachusetts
Toronto

Library of Congress Cataloging in Publication Data

Main entry under title:

Faculty and teacher bargaining.
    Includes index.
    1. Teachers' unions—United States—Addresses, essays, lectures.
2. Collective bargaining—Teachers—United States—Addresses, essays,
lectures. I. Title.
LB2844.53.U6F33   331.88'113711'00973   80-8769
ISBN 0-669-04360-5

Published simultaneously in Canada

Printed in the United States of America

International Standard Book Number: 0-669-04360-5

Library of Congress Catalog Card Number: 80-8769

Contents

Foreword

American education is in the middle of an attenuated struggle to make peace with itself about teacher unionization. At a time of substantial economic humiliation of teachers and nearly a half-century after the National Labor Relations Act, some observers wonder why so many of those concerned with the educating professions are still antagonistic to and fearful of unionization. Still others view the very idea of teachers' unions as a dire threat to professionalism and collegiality, often considered the hallmarks of dignity and status in educational careers.

Compared with the long history of trade unionism in the United States, teachers' unions are a recent phenomenon. Although their beginnings can be traced to 1916, when the American Federation of Teachers was founded and chartered by the American Federation of Labor, the real development of teachers' unions in the United States came in the 1960s—spectacularly in grades K-12, sporadically in postsecondary education.[a] Why teachers' unions emerged when they emerged and in the form that they did is closely related to the history of the American labor movement generally and to recent social and economic history specifically.

Labor unions in the United States and throughout the world began as an organized protest of workers against low pay and intolerable working conditions. Organized first by individual crafts (for example, carpenters, printers, shoemakers, and masons) in specific localities, local specialized unions—influenced by patent communities of interest—coalesced into larger, more general organizations. So, for example, as early as 1827 a combination of local crafts formed the Mechanics Union of Trade Associations in Philadelphia. It is important to add, however, that coalitions have not snowballed symmetrically. There has been no inexorable and consistent drift toward an overarching labor unity in the past century and a half. To the contrary, labor movements in the United States have been marked by fluctuating internal divisions and by alternating periods of growth and decline. America, unlike many European nations, has never developed a major political party built predominantly upon a labor base. The only time that seemed even remotely conceivable was in the troubled period after the Civil War, when the Noble Order of the Knights of Labor developed a political saliency of substantial proportions—featuring among its goals the abolition of child labor and the institution of an eight-hour day. But hordes of immigrants and a growing antiradical national mood soon decimated the ranks of the Knights of Labor. In its place, nearly a half-century ago, unions of skilled workers formed the American Federation of Labor (AFL) whose leader, Samuel

---

[a]The NEA was organized in 1857 as the National Teachers Association, but it did not take on the characteristics of a trade union until the early 1960s.

Gompers, placed an indelible stamp of pragmatism and incrementalism on the future of American trade unionism. The goal of the AFL was not to become a labor party but to win "more" for each unionized worker. The chief instrument for achieving that "more" was collective bargaining made vital by adversary proceedings and the "right to strike" and by adherence to a pragmatic political doctrine of "support your friends and defeat your enemies."

By 1900 the AFL had more than a half-million members. Twenty years later that number had grown to 4 million. Not included, however, were millions of semiskilled and unskilled workers, white-collar workers, and uniformed public employees. The first group began to coalesce into the Congress of Industrial Organizations (CIO) in the 1930s. The second and third groups became increasingly unionized after World War II. But the right of public employees to strike—especially those in organizations affecting the public safety and health—has been and still is hotly debated. It is often forgotten that the election of Calvin Coolidge as president of the United States in 1924 was in part attributable to his having broken the Boston police strike in 1919 when he was governor of Massachusetts.

During the middle years of the twentieth century, unionism in the United States was marked by an increasingly large measure of legal acceptance. But it was also marked by extended intramural struggles and by highly ambivalent public attitudes. Every time there seemed to be a real possibility of achieving a united labor movement, the personal chemistries of leaders and divergent economic and political interests got in the way. The uneasy relationship between craft unions and industrial unions has never been totally resolved. Blue-collar and white-collar workers still feel uneasy with one another. Racism has been a divisive force. And underneath it all has been a widespread public ambivalence toward unionism—a grudging recognition of its importance in containing exploitation by domineering employers, but a fear (partly cultivated by employer groups) of union power and an ineffable① sense that individualism, not collective action, had been the driving historic force in releasing America's economic might.

It is not surprising, granted this background, that when teachers began to organize seriously in the 1960s they viewed the world through the historic eyes of the American labor movement, with its emphasis on collective bargaining, the sanctity of the right to strike, economic incrementalism, and political pragmatism. Nor is it any wonder that the emergence of teachers' unions was viewed by the general public with some trepidation and even hostility. The all-too-frequent image of the teacher as a selfless mendicant who disdained worldly goods and whose only motivations and rewards were associated with the dedicated pursuit of a professional calling was rudely shattered by signs on a picket line during an "illegal" strike demanding decent pay and dignified treatment. But the enormous demand for teachers occasioned by the postwar baby boom and by new educational expectations of individuals and of an

① incapable of being expressed in words

increasingly complex economy gave teachers an inherent bargaining power that they had lacked in previous decades.

In the 1960s and 1970s teachers became organized but not united. True to the larger template of American unionism, teachers found it impossible to develop a united front. The American Federation of Teachers (AFT), with its close ideological and organizational ties to blue-collar unionism, seemed "antiprofessional" to members of the National Education Association (NEA). The latter seemed to AFT militants to represent company unionism at its worst. At the postsecondary level, the American Association of University Professors (AAUP) had maintained a kind of gentle squatters' rights in the higher academy. Most of its members found the prospect of an uncollegial unionization of faculty as abhorrent as it seemed redundant. By the early 1970s, when elementary and secondary teachers had become heavily unionized (the NEA by then quite as collective-bargaining oriented as the AFT), only a small fraction of postsecondary faculties had formed unions, and most of these were in public systems, especially in community colleges. But postsecondary unionization among faculty members expanded rapidly through the 1970s so that by 1980 more than 43 percent of all faculty members in higher education were represented by unions. The overwhelming proportion of these were in the public sector. The 1980s will see continuing efforts to unionize colleges and universities, and the process will most likely be messy. A more militant AAUP will be struggling to maintain its position against both the AFT and the NEA. Increasingly, existing state collective-bargaining laws are being extended to include all public employees, including publicly supported teachers, and new laws are being passed. In private higher education, the future is clouded—partly because of the *Yeshiva* case (1980) in which the Supreme Court ruled that where faculty play various management roles in a university setting, they cannot be considered employees for purposes of collective bargaining. Repercussions of the *Yeshiva* case may be felt in both the private and the public sectors.

This cursory history simply underscores the obvious point that few issues in the field of American education have been more controversial in the past two decades than the rise of teachers' unions. Struggles over appropriate bargaining agents, what issues are negotiable, grievance procedures, the right to strike, and even the underlying compatibility of unions and the educating professions have divided faculty, outraged administrators, politicized schools and colleges, entangled the courts, and roiled public opinion.

Yet, strangely, very little is known about the impact of unionism on the educational process and on educational outcomes. For this reason, the National Academy of Education, with support from the Ford Foundation, commissioned a series of essays on unionization and education. Dr. George Angell, former college president and former director of the Academic Collective Bargaining Information Service in Washington, D.C., kindly consented to organize and edit such a volume and to contribute the lead essay, "Faculty Bargaining in American

Higher Education, 1960–1980." Dr. Angell, in turn, asked a number of informed and experienced colleagues to write critical responses to his essay. He also asked Robert E. Doherty, associate dean for academic affairs at the New York State School of Industrial and Labor Relations, Cornell University, and an expert on problems of bargaining in public education, to prepare a major essay on K–12 unionism. This essay, too, was subjected to critical reviews by a number of informed and experienced commentators.

No punches have been pulled. This book is filled with spirited disagreements on matters of fact, value, and judgment. The Academy mandate was not to have contributors conduct original research (although one of the major values of the essays is to remind us of how little we really know about this tangled area). The Academy's hope was that a number of informed and experienced people might provide for the attentive public a photomontage of views about what unionization is actually doing to American education at all levels. Dr. Angell and his colleagues have responded with vigor and with uncommon insight.

The Academy is grateful to all of them and is proud to make their collective views available to all those in our society who, like Academy members, are concerned with "the ends and means of education in all its forms in the United States and abroad" (National Academy of Education Charter).

Stephen K. Bailey
President, National Academy of Education

1 Faculty Bargaining in American Higher Education, 1960–1980

George W. Angell

Roots of Faculty Bargaining

Writers generally ascribe specific causes to the advent of faculty bargaining in America. Among causes commonly listed are relatively low compensation of teachers, arbitrary and capricious institutional practices, lack of faculty prestige and power in academic matters, and the legalization of collective bargaining for public-college employees in twenty-four states. Indeed, these conditions provoked faculty interest in unionization but were not the only causes. Presence of enabling state legislation always seemed to be accompanied by faculty elections and bargaining, while its absence in southern and midsouthern states appears to be a monumental obstacle to the unionization of public-college faculties. Yet in some areas, notably Ohio, Illinois, Nevada, and the District of Columbia, lack of legislation has not prevented faculty unions from appearing at a number of public universities. Of interest also is the fact that many faculties, especially at private colleges, burdened with low salaries and little campus influence, have made almost no significant move toward unionization. These and other considerations lead me to believe that the larger forces of tradition and social change may be worthy of more attention than heretofore given as causes of the upswing in faculty bargaining during the late sixties and seventies.

In a sense faculties have always bargained with institutional management on matters of salary, employment policies, and academic freedom. The early existence of faculty senates and advisory councils indicates that higher education executives, long before the advent of unions, consulted their faculties not only for information but as a means of avoiding or defusing mass reaction to unpopular

---

Editor's note: It is important for the reader to understand that the essays herein are just that, essays, not research reports. The National Academy of Education (NAEd) asked us to think about faculty bargaining, its roots and purposes, its effects and future. Although each writer necessarily draws heavily from experience and research, the thrust of each piece is to extrapolate beyond available data in search of a broader interpretation of the phenomenon and to suggest future developments and actions that may be beneficial to the educational enterprise. The task of prediction is fraught with well-known dangers, not the least of which is the irrepressible urge to pontificate, exhort, and admonish, usually along lines of personal bias, however subtle. Since the writers have had differing types of experiences, variations in biases, it is hoped, provide some balance. Yet to accomplish the purpose of the task, we felt it important that each point of view be left to stand on its merit to provoke the total range of reactions both positive and negative.

decisions or inadequate conditions. Systematic consultation and collective action, however weak, constitute in my view a bona-fide form of early collective bargaining. In colleges and universities this type of joint action among professional employees and employers was so unique to colleges that it was called *collegiality*. In some private institutions the collegium was, and still is, vested by charter and other documents of incorporation with legal status and authority. Although legal authority for faculty governance existed at some of the early public institutions, it was not as common as at the more prestigious private universities. Institutions failing to provide legal status for faculty governance often became the early battlegrounds for academic freedom and faculty power. More important for this essay, they became the scenes of faculty collective action demanding changes in academic and employment policies. As a result of concerted pressure, it became common for trustees and/or administration to establish some form of collegial structure as an advisory body It was not unusual, however, for administrators to act in a manner contrary to the advice of faculty, and whenever this happened, it was only natural for faculties to seek legal authority to prevent future unilateral decisions. As an example, twenty-three years after the New York State Legislature founded Cornell University, the trustees, under pressure from faculty, passed a resolution that required the president to obtain a nomination by the faculty senate before a new professor could be appointed. Later the faculty lobbied the New York State Legislature, and this quasi-legal status of the faculty was incorporated into university legislation.[1] This action does not appear to me to be too different from that of a faculty today turning to the trustees or to a labor board for the right to organize and bargain with the administration relative to faculty appointments and other conditions of employment.

A parallel movement among industrial employees finally reached public acceptance in the form of the Wagner Act (NLRA) of 1935, which in 1970, by a decision of the National Labor Relations Board (NLRB), was extended to employees of private colleges and universities. Traditions of political independence and professional pride, however, delayed faculty acceptance of trade unionism. Few faculty members prior to 1975 viewed industrial bargaining as being even remotely related to collegial bargaining. Thus the idea of a faculty unionizing to attain its collegial rights had to await the social forces unleashed by the widespread abhorrence of the Vietnam war and the arbitrary and capricious acts of government officials at the highest levels. The long-subdued struggles of the unenfranchised, such as blacks and students, coalesced by 1968 into a national uprising against unresponsive authority. The advent of this movement could not have come at a time more opportune for engendering interest and support among academics. During the late fifties and sixties college enrollments dramatically expanded, creating thousands of faculty vacancies for which there were relatively few candidates qualified by advanced study, research, and teaching experience. Vacancies were filled primarily by youthful graduate students and others lacking the usual initiation into the traditions of academe. It was generally the young and uninitiated faculty members who led campus rebellions of the sixties against entrenched authority, especially at two-year public colleges that had yet to develop substantive collegial structures. The struggle for faculty power was not new, but the anti-Vietnam War fever, if it may be called that, infused unenfranchised faculties with new energy, ideas, and determination. Within a decade faculties almost everywhere had won more power by (1) persuading trustees and administrators to either strengthen collegial governance or to permit faculty unionization under trustee-determined regulations[2] or by (2) electing, under law, a bargaining agent. Thus expansion of collegiality and unionization developed simultaneously as means for achieving overlapping objectives. Some collegial structures, by accepting a realistic role in determining conditions of employment, often made unionization unnecessary. At the same time a faculty union, once established on a campus, either displaced or strengthened existing weak collegial structures by negotiating a contract that provided legal authority as a basis for faculty participation in campus governance. Thus I see faculty bargaining as an integral part of the historical movement toward collegial management of academic affairs. Charter-based faculty collegiums are, in my view, prototype unions that bargain a wide scope of issues that go beyond, but include, conditions of employment. It is not unusual, as an example, for a faculty senate to have considerable influence relative to such matters as educational programs, appointment of administrators, and broad institutional policy generally beyond the legal scope of union bargaining. On the other hand, unions develop political action and power at the local, state, and national levels where faculty senates are generally impotent and uninterested. In my view these differences will all but disappear in the nineties since the central mission of both groups is to secure academic freedom, faculty governance, and institutional viability. Unions to date have not shown much interest in pursuing academic excellence as a basis for job security, but I believe this will change. If and when this change occurs, there will be fewer barriers to merging collegial and union forces. In other words, I believe that the debate as to the validity of unionism on campus is for all intent and purpose over. The questions now become, "How fast will faculty unionism spread to new campuses?", "To what extent can some measure of national faculty unity be achieved?", and, "Will unions and college administrators ever work together toward institutional goals of excellence and service?"

Current Status of Unions

Roughly speaking, 700 of 3,000, or 23 percent, of the nation's campuses have faculties that bargain collectively for conditions of employment. Unions represent approximately 50 percent (150,000 of 300,000) of all college teachers in America. This is a much larger proportion than the 22 percent of the total American workforce represented by union agents.[3] And the proportion is growing each year. Three key indicators predict that faculty unions will continue the expansion achieved in the seventies. First is the success of their political efforts to pass enabling legislation in states where it has not existed and to amend existing laws. A second predictor is the number of faculties that requests and wins union elections under existing laws. From the midsixties to January 1980, agent elections were held at 501 institutions, and 401 faculties elected unions.[4] In addition, there was in 1979 an increase in the number of faculties at small private colleges requesting NLRB to conduct elections.

A third predictor is the relative absence of decertification of existing faculty unions. Spread of bargaining in the industrial sector has been seriously hampered by employees who decide for a variety of reasons to vote local unions out of existence. As an example, about 600 separate employee groups in 1978 voted to oust their union agents.[5] In the history of higher education, only two faculties, both at small rural campuses, have decertified without replacing their agents.[6] On the other hand, faculty unions easily rebuffed the only two determined efforts by antiunion forces at large university sites.[7] Other efforts at decertification such as the one at the University of Hawaii have largely been aimed at selecting a new agent who might be more effective in attaining faculty objectives. These of course are not the only predictors, but all three indicate continuance and growth of formal negotiations by college and university faculties. Speculation as to whether or not unions will ever become common at prestigious graduate universities is probably not too important since faculties at those institutions are already powerful and regularly bargain with administration relative to matters of interest to them. Faculties at Rutgers, Temple, and The City University of New York are examples of graduate faculties that already exercise both collegial and union power. The election campaigns shaping at the University of California campuses, if won by the unions, may change the earlier image that faculties at prestigious campuses are not interested in unionization.

Success of Faculty Unions

To address the issue of faculty-union success requires some effort at generalizing union objectives. Obviously each campus had a unique set of conditions leading to a union election, and to assess a measure of success at a particular campus would necessitate definition of those conditions and the promises made by the eventual winner during the election campaign. Beyond this uniqueness, however, one cannot help but be impressed by the commonality of union objectives whether expressed in campaign literature or in the professional journals. For purposes of this paper it appears to be sufficient and appropriate to identify six of the most frequently stated goals.

1. To increase salaries and fringe benefits.
2. To establish orderly procedures that would reasonably assure equitable treatment of members relative to salary, promotions, tenure, and other conditions of employment.
3. To expand the influence of faculty recommendations in those procedures.
4. To improve the professional status of faculty members, especially at those institutions that provided few of the profession's perquisites such as sabbatic leaves, faculty senates, "reasonable" workloads, research assistance, and protection of academic freedom. (An exception should be noted here. At some institutions faculties may have unionized to help preserve status, for example, a law-school faculty might have unionized separately to prevent being locked into campuswide salary and work schedules, or a single campus might unionize in an attempt to avoid being absorbed into a statewide faculty organization.)
5. To establish a grievance procedure that provides protection against arbitrary and/or capricious personnel decisions.
6. To establish direct contact and influence with top-level decision makers. (This applies primarily at large universities and at campuses within a multicampus system.)

If these six items represent a reasonably accurate statement of union objectives across the nation, I would have to conclude that most unions have been successful. Although studies comparing salaries at unionized and nonunionized campuses have been widely criticized for technical deficiencies, the weight of evidence indicates that unions, especially during the initial years of negotiation, have clearly improved salaries and fringe benefits. It is important to note, however, that there is no evidence to my knowledge that unionized faculties have increased the total funding of their institutions, even in public higher education where union political clout with legislatures might be expected to make a difference. As an example, nonunionized public institutions in Ohio, Michigan, Montana, and Oregon appear to receive appropriations equal to those of their unionized counterparts. To be fair, unions seldom, if ever, promise to increase salaries only by larger appropriations. In fact, during election campaigns union representatives ordinarily declare that faculty salaries should receive a higher priority within existing budgets. To my knowledge this higher priority has usually been achieved, the few exceptions being in situations where state law or trustee policy limits the scope of salary bargaining to funds specifically appropriated by government for salaries and fringe benefits. Yet in the long run, I believe that total institutional funding will necessarily become of more interest to unions as they mature and broaden their purposes.

One merely needs to select at random a few union-negotiated contracts and compare them with institutional personnel policies of the preunion days to come to the conclusion that unions have been uniformly successful in establishing more orderly personnel procedures that depend on effective faculty participation. Also almost every contract accords faculty members the basic perquisites generally expected by the profession. A nonmoney item commonly negotiated into contracts is a grievance procedure that, as a rule, provides a binding final-step decision by either a neutral adjudicator or a panel balanced in terms of partisanship.

This leaves for discussion union objective number 6, and there is little doubt about its achievement. Faculty representatives at the State University of New York, as an example, bargain directly with the governor's Office of Employee Relations, thus by-passing even the university system's chancellor. State college faculties in Pennsylvania bargain directly with the state's secretary of education. The faculties of the New Jersey state college system have been successful on occasion in obtaining the help of the governor in overriding the actions of the system's chancellor. In Montana each campus union negotiates with a management team chaired by the chancellor's negotiator. It is probably fair to say that systemwide bargaining substantially increases faculty visibility and influence at the highest levels of decision making in both political and educational arenas. Local campus bargaining, however, will do this only when government is represented at the negotiation table, as is often the case during community college negotiations.

Other Effects of Faculty Bargaining

Although campus unions seldom express official aspirations beyond the six objectives noted, they are often credited with a number of side-effects that go well beyond immediate goals. One such effect is the general pressure that unionized faculties exert on many, if not all, nonunionized campuses. Nonunionized faculties expect to receive treatment at least equal to their unionized brethren and make their feelings known at propitious times. Unfortunately, few college presidents conceal their abhorrence of the possibility that union organizers may come to campus. Most admit privately that they do everything possible to keep unions off campus including the improvement of salaries, perquisites, and personnel procedures. In general, unions appear to have had more effect than they would like on nonunionized campuses because the job of union expansion is made much more difficult by competitive benefits at campuses where faculty members do not have to pay union dues.

During visits to unionized campuses, I usually ask administrators about the effects of faculty bargaining on administrative work. To date every administrator questioned has admitted that negotiation requires much more attention to structure and detail, especially in matters of promotion, tenure, merit salary increases, and grievance review. And they say that this leads generally to more careful planning, budgeting, record keeping, data processing, dialogue with faculty representatives, and personnel procedures. Despite these admissions,

few administrators are willing to say that their institutions are better administered than they were prior to faculty bargaining. What I gather from their
comments is that they believe the use of technical devices for improving personnel procedures was merely speeded up by negotiations and that good administration is built on the kinds of human relationships that are often lost, or
at least very difficult to maintain, within a bargaining-contractual-adversary
relationship. Administrators are not very clear about just what constitutes
those human relationships, but they extol the virtues of a one-on-one relationship unfettered by unnecessary restrictions. Union representatives, on the
other hand, point out that it was precisely this one-on-one situation that made
many faculty members feel powerless in discussions with administrators. Feelings among administrators who work with unionized faculties run the gamut
from outright hatred of unions to a reasonable acceptance of unions as a fact
of life. Those who accept the concept of faculty unionism, in my judgment,
represent less than 10 percent and perhaps less than 5 percent of the total.
Yet my general impression is that faculty bargaining has had a salutary effect
on management procedures if not on faculty-administrator relationships.

Another impression is that an executive who arrives on campus a year
or more after the union election is less likely to be negative about the union
presence than the executive who experienced an election campaign directed
at remedying conditions for which he or she was responsible. This impression,
if accurate, may not be too important in this decade, but it may have signifi-
cance in the decades ahead when fewer administrators will have experienced
an election campaign and will be more ready psychologically to make the
most of opportunities offered by the union presence on campus.

Still another impression is that union leadership generally appears to be
pleased that college administrators have deep anxiety about, if not outright
fear of, faculty organization. It seems to me that this phenomenon should
be considered carefully by national unions that carry much of the responsibility
for creating this mutual antipathy. They should ask themselves whether or not
such effects are helpful to their long-range purposes. Hatred of unions by industrial managers has become a major obstacle to union growth. The real question
that national education unions must ask themselves is whether it is not time
to work more cooperatively with administrators once a union becomes established and gains a measure of security on campus. It seems imperative that
both administrators and unions seek mutual understanding and respect through
which they can share common concerns for educational excellence. This
mature relationship has been at least partially achieved at places such as Temple
and Southeastern Massachusetts Universities.

Another side-effect of faculty bargaining is a tendency to involve external
political power as an arbiter of campus issues. At public colleges faculty
bargaining in time may become a purely political exercise. An example is a
community college that is sponsored and partially financed by a county. Faculty

representatives frequently bargain directly with elected county officials and/or their counsel. This immediately brings elected officials and their political colleagues into discussions of tenure, promotions, merit salary, college calendar, sabbatic leaves, and other matters related to educational program and academic freedom. This may not be bad, yet it is well known that politicians cannot over-look the political consequences of their bargains with faculty and that their positions on issues may be oriented more toward political than educational outcomes. Furthermore, faculty unions can develop considerable political clout by campaigning in an election period for candidates likely to be agreeable at the bargaining table. In a sense, unions may control, rather than simply bargain with, management. Such a maneuver defeats the very meaning of bargaining between equals. At state-supported institutions, the effects are similar except that state officials and state politics are involved. Where this occurs, it is not unusual for a governor to intervene directly in state university matters that affect him politically. To be fair, this has always been true, but prior to bargaining, intervention was rare and carefully considered lest it arouse the opposition of the academic community. Bargaining actually legitimizes the intervention and provides periodic academic-political forums.

The political overtones of faculty bargaining at a private university are less blatant since trustees, rather than government, are the policymakers who employ and direct the executive branch of the university. Nevertheless, it is not unusual for trustees to become targets for faculty politics, and sometimes university presidents become middlemen or mediators in an attempt to achieve agreement between the parties. More than one president has complained that trustees are more difficult to bargain with than the faculty. The net effect on some, if not most presidencies, is that a higher priority is placed on the skills of mediation than on matters of education. This is equally true at public institu-tions except that the institution's president must extend his efforts daily into the field of public politics or accept a minor role as a branch manager of a campus. Interestingly enough, some presidents seem to "grow and glow" under the twin spotlights of politics and publicity while others retreat. Those who have retreated appear to me, by and large, to be intellectually at least the equal of those who enjoy the political arena. More important to education is the fact that administrative retreat leaves the university open to a biased type of negotia-tion between faculty representatives and politicians, whereby management concerns and responsibility are seldom represented fully and accurately. Faculty union representatives are not accountable for protecting management's authority for long-range planning, for developing new programs, for cutting back on ineffective programs, for disengaging faculty members who are ineffective or whose services are no longer needed, or for holding down the rising costs of education. Politicians, having little insight into the interrelatedness of faculty-student-administrative functions, are eager to strike a bargain that is politically feasible. The effects of such bargains on the quality of education are not quickly visible, but the long-range consequences could be devastating to managerial effectiveness. One observable result at some campuses has been a steady decrease in percentage of funds allocated for such services as faculty research, student assistantships, secretarial services, new equipment, inservice-training programs for faculty and administrators, faculty and administrative travel, and for institutional research. It takes years for educational deterioration to become obvious, but my experience indicates that an untraveled faculty is likely to become an immutable faculty and that a faculty lacking incentive for research will sooner or later consider higher education as the accumulation of factual knowledge. Either can destroy the meaning and vitality of the academy. It is hoped that faculty unions will some day be able to bargain salary agreements that will "outrun" inflation and then perhaps they will be willing to fight persistently and effectively for the total educational budget.

But one goal they may never be willing to bargain for is a more effective administration, that is, one with adequate staff, salaries, prestige, and authority. It is here that most faculty-versus-politician bargaining is almost totally blind. Faculties and governments expect aggressive, effective educational leadership on every campus, but they do not evaluate their negotiators in terms of the extent to which a contract strengthens or weakens administrative services. In fact, many politicians, especially legislators, see their own goals as being more consonant with faculty satisfaction than with administrative effectiveness. The net result appears to me to be a slow but general deterioration in the salary, responsibility, authority, and prestige of college administrators, especially at campuses where chief executives have little control over the bargaining processes. One emerging effect at such campuses in the late seventies appeared to be less desire by college officials to take a stand on tough issues, for example, to make long-range plans that showed imagination and courage, to forge ahead with new programs that maintain or increase enrollments, to insist on high standards for employing, promoting, and tenuring faculty, and to terminate ineffective or inefficient programs. If this view has any validity, the future vitality of such campuses will decline until faculty unions awaken to the gravity of mediocre management and resist the temptation to undercut at the bargaining table the authority and importance of their administrative colleagues. Faculty members to whom I have spoken about this rarely show concern. It is their general view that they can do better with less administration, leaving the hard decisions to the faculty collegium. My own observations and experience lead me to believe that this would be a serious mistake. A faculty without leadership is likely to become aimless and unresponsive to change, a condition leading to institutional deterioration followed by severe reform or extinction.

Faculty bargaining has also affected the roles of governing boards. When negotiations occur at a four-year campus, whether it is public or private, the trustees are likely to become directly or indirectly involved in the issues of bargaining and to be more informed about college affairs. When the bargaining occurs away from campus on a systemwide basis, trustees are less likely to become involved and usually lose jurisdiction over conditions of faculty employment. Trustee involvement at two-year colleges also decreases wherever systemwide bargaining is practiced and especially when government agents other than campus administrators control bargaining processes. Many public colleges suffer the consequences of inconsistent legislation whereby education law empowers trustees to establish personnel policy and conditions of faculty employment, but public-employment law enables faculties to bargain conditions of employment directly with government employers other than trustees. This legal confusion is a continuing source of friction between trustees and government officials. Where the friction is severe, effective management is extremely difficult because college presidents are forced to report, in a sense, to two masters, each holding jurisdiction over differing but related parts of the budget and institutional operations. The educational consequences are too complex and emerge too slowly to be predictable at this time, but they are certain to exist and should be of concern to everyone. The most dangerous outcome, it seems to me, is the loss of definitive responsibility. When trustees, campus executives, union leaders and political-office holders can, with some validity, blame each other for lack of educational effectiveness yet claim the right to share in the important decisions, the willingness to make difficult decisions will wane and so will the institution's vitality. The answer to this dilemma is to change the labor law in a manner that recognizes the trustees as the legal public employer as established by education law. In states where I have suggested this remedy, there has been little support. Unions want to negotiate directly with those who hold political and economic power. Political-office holders do not wish to relinquish their new power over educational institutions. Trustees and college presidents are afraid to buck political-office holders upon whom they depend for appropriations. Yet I am convinced that it can and should be done. Politicians are generally people of goodwill who have, time and again, made difficult decisions on behalf of higher education. Here again, it will take aggressive and intelligent university leadership to lead the trustees in a political battle for the university's independence.

Has faculty bargaining increased the cost of educational services? Yes, if one believes college administrators who cite the costs of negotiations, new personnel officers, sophisticated data processing, low faculty loads in low-enrollment programs, featherbedding practices, excessive grievance processing, and high faculty compensation. In addition, the cost of huge amounts of time required of academic administrators for union dialogue, contract administration, and grievance processing are recited. To these are added the costs of incalculable amounts of faculty time given to union rather than educational affairs. Union spokesmen counter effectively with arguments that union negotiation merely replaces the time-consuming, ineffective practices of faculty-administrative committees that formerly conducted the same business in a less orderly manner producing untold grievances that festered for years without final resolution. Although unions agree that they have negotiated more dollar benefits for their members, they feel that much if not all of the difference in compensation paid to faculty is recovered by better distribution of institutional funds and a reduction in unnecessary managerial services. Both parties argue sincerely and persuasively, but with the aid of few hard facts. A look at industrial bargaining over a period of time longer than that offered by faculty bargaining makes one wonder whether or not a nonunionized company such as International Business Machines may spend more money attempting to avoid unionization than it would have to spend to accommodate bargaining. If this is true, cost is not IBM's primary concern relative to the issue of collective bargaining. Likewise, cost does not appear to be a prime concern of legislators who pass labor laws. Except for the matter raised earlier about the redistribution of educational funds in a manner that may seriously reduce faculty travel, research and other educationally related services, I see little point in attempting to evaluate the arguments about cost.

In a more general context, one might inquire about the impact of faculty bargaining on the means and ends of education. Most of the answers offered by union or management about this larger question seem specious. Unions generally argue that better salaries and working conditions will attract and hold a better-qualified faculty. Administrators say that union protection tends to decrease faculty interest in maintaining high professional standards in developing new programs and in giving extra class time to students. There is probably some evidence to support the arguments of each, but the tests of time and hard research are yet to come. My general assessment is that faculty bargaining has had little impact on the means of education that I generally classify under such rubrics as the quality of the faculty, of the student body, of the laboratories and libraries, and the availability of resources. Obviously then there appears to be as yet little effect on the ends of higher education such as the quality and performance of graduates, the research of faculty members, and other public services performed by the university.

Keys to the Future

The future character and quality of faculty bargaining is in the hands of several groups of people whose efforts are more often a series of reactions to each other than a sustained pursuit of humanistic purpose. Coming events therefore must be perceived in terms of several factors before a reasoned guess about the whole can be pieced together.

Future Legislation Related to Faculty Bargaining

My contacts with administrators, trustees, union representatives, and legislators in several regions of the country predict that attention to labor legislation in every state of the union, with the exception perhaps of North Carolina, is increasing every year. Washington, Ohio, and Wisconsin have been debating bills and shaping legislation for several years. They are likely to pass new laws during the eighties. Several states that now have meet-and-confer laws are feeling strong pressures for bona-fide labor legislation requiring written agreements between parties. National unions have aided local and state associations of teachers in developing political campaigns for legislation in every state. These efforts, by and large, are planned carefully to create a favorable political climate prior to final legislation. Powerful political allies, for example, the American Federation of State, City and Municipal Employees, also press for comprehensive public-employee legislation. Tradition now seems to favor extension of labor rights to public employees everywhere. Twenty-four states already permit faculty bargaining in public higher education. Several of these state laws have been on the books more than ten years and have been amended time and again to achieve more balance of power at the bargaining table. During this trial period there has been almost no serious challenge toward repealing existing legislation. An additional six to ten states will probably pass enabling legislation during the eighties. Consequently, by 1990, 60 to 70 percent of all faculty members are likely to be represented by unions. In two-year colleges where unions win more than 80 percent of agent elections, the percentage will be higher. These predictions may not hold should the current trend toward political conservatism and other forces, discussed later, exert influence stronger than that of enabling legislation.

Similarly, Congress, which has already approved a new Department of Education, will be under severe pressure to broaden the coverage of the National Labor Relations Act (NLRA) to include state employees and additional groups of privately employed workers, for example, hospital employees were recently included by amendment. Observation of certain congressional committees and their staff members over the last several years suggests that nothing is likely to deter them from attempting to extend coverage of NLRA and, in addition, to broaden the scope of bargaining to include the impact of all managerial decisions on conditions of employment. Congress and NLRB are carefully observing the case law developing around state legislation. Yet it is my guess that actual passage of NLRA amendments will come slowly because there will be a trend toward conservatism in a Congress made wary by inflation, recession, Proposition 13, Supreme Court rulings, and the 1980 elections. Nevertheless, congressional committee activity on such matters as coverage of state employees will in itself encourage passage of laws by states anxious to avoid possible federal intervention.

One other phenomenon, faculty bargaining under trustee regulation, should be mentioned in connection with possible passage of new legislation. Teachers in higher education are learning that in the absence of enabling legislation, it is still possible to persuade trustees to permit faculty bargaining under trustee-established regulations. This practice is gaining respect and credibility in Ohio and Illinois and was the forerunner of legislation in states such as Washington and Michigan. This type of bargaining, in the absence of regulation by state labor agencies, is conducted entirely within campus-governing processes and appears to preserve the advantages of university self-governance reasonably independent of state politics. It would be a useful experiment for a state to pass a labor law that reaffirms the independent nature of university self-governance as established by education law. One way to do this would be to pass a public-employee bargaining law that exempted public higher education from its jurisdiction, noting that education law has established boards of trustees as the legislative bodies governing institutions of higher learning. Such a law would state that the trustees have responsibility to determine whether or not collective bargaining is to be preferred to other methods of conducting employment relations with faculties. In my view this arrangement would affirm education law by requiring the academic community, as a self-governing constituency, to seek its own remedies to labor issues. It would also go a long way in preserving the political independence of the university. From a pragmatic point of view, however, I do not expect that college presidents and trustees will be able to generate the unity, organization, and influence necessary to effect such an outcome. Nevertheless, it seems important to suggest that both parties study the successful bargaining at a number of campuses now bargaining under trustee regulation.[8]

Court Decisions

Faculty bargaining has obviously been affected by court decisions relative to issues of tenure, promotions, salary and the scope of bargaining. The net interpretation that I place on a decade of such decisions is that courts seem to be extending the Bill of Rights into many areas of employment.[9] Although the intent of the Bill of Rights was to protect each citizen from unwarranted aggression by government, it is obvious that courts will now protect an employee from an employer's action that has the effect of discrimination. The concept of equal protection in employment practices places, as it should, a special burden on academics who are required to judge their colleagues on such elusive qualities as teaching effectiveness, research, and public service. To end discrimination, educators must attempt to substantiate academic decisions that prior to 1960 were seldom challenged in courts of law. Effects of court decisions on campus operations are not dissimilar to those of faculty bargaining, for example, more attention to detailed records, procedures, and consultation prior to personnel decisions. Two decades of scrutiny by the courts is reducing the number of arbitrary, capricious, and/or discriminatory decisions upon which union-election campaigns often depend for success. In other words, government efforts to eliminate discrimination may substantially reduce the need for faculties to unionize in the future.

Court decisions relative to other issues also affect the spread of faculty bargaining. In 1976 the Supreme Court decided that overtime provisions of the federal minimum-wage law shall not apply to people employed by a state or its political subdivisions since it would constitute unwarranted intrusion in matters constitutionally delegated to the states.[10] This decision had a chilling, but not fatal, effect on union efforts to extend jurisdiction of NLRA to state employees. In addition, the Supreme Court in February 1980 decided the Yeshiva University case, which may be the landmark decision of the century relative to faculty bargaining in private colleges. In a split decision, the Court upheld an earlier decision by the U.S. Court of Appeals to the effect that Yeshiva faculty members do not qualify as employees under NLRA since they share substantial managerial authority and function.[11] This decision will have far-reaching effects on faculty bargaining. As an example, state-by-state consideration of the ruling could delay new state legislation enabling faculty bargaining. In addition, any private college seriously wishing to avoid faculty unionization may attempt to simulate conditions at Yeshiva sufficiently to disqualify its faculty members as employees. Thus court rulings could become a major influence on the rate at which faculty unionization under law proceeds in the eighties.

It appears to me, however, that when a university disqualifies its faculty members as employees by increasing their collective decision-making authority via faculty senates and departmental committees, it strengthens and legitimizes an intracampus faculty-bargaining relationship. It is my contention that these bargaining relationships, formal and informal, under trustee policy will continue to grow in the eighties and nineties to the point where virtually every accredited institution of higher education in the United States will, in effect, be negotiating with its collective faculty in one form or another. Both types of bargaining produce written contracts. Collegial-type bargaining produces a set of printed policies that are enforced through internal grievance mechanisms. Such policies usually cover a range of subjects equal to or broader than those included in union contracts.

Public Attitudes toward Unions

The dramatic rise in the unionization of public employees has increased public debate over the pros and cons of unions. One report indicates that some union officials agree with polls that show that public-employee strikes, especially among fire fighters, police, and teachers, are seriously affecting public opinion about unions in general and strikes in particular. In addition, negative public opinion is generated by increased publicity given to high union-wage settlements and their effects on inflation. More and more attention is also directed to the fact that foreign imports can undersell U.S. goods because of the high domestic union-labor costs. Negative public opinion is a strong deterrent to the passage of new state and federal legislation favorable to unions.[12]

Another concern that could chill the spread of unionism is a possible public demand for wage-and-price controls. War or severe inflation could bring nationwide wage-and-price controls that usually reduce the effectiveness of and interest in collective bargaining. Two local forms of wage control are the prevailing-rate system and coalition bargaining. Prevailing rates, as used by the city of San Francisco, tie wages and benefits to those already established in neighboring and similar locations. More and more states and cities are, without admitting it, using a type of internal prevailing-wage system whereby the employer bargains first with the group of employees most likely to settle at the lowest compensation and then declares the resulting wage settlement as the rate for all other groups. Much has been said, mostly negative, about the fact that New York City, by bargaining with as many as 177 different unions, sustains an exceedingly high cost of negotiations, constant turmoil (one or more unions always seem to be on strike), differing rates of salary increases within overlapping contractual periods, and the resulting whipsawing that appears to drive wages higher than the public may approve. Negative public opinion created by unfavorable publicity could bring a new wave of demands for the use of coalition bargaining (in a sense, bargaining with all unions simultaneously), prevailing rates, or even plebiscites to determine salary increases over fixed periods of time. All such actions could chill the spread of unions.

On the other hand, several other public-opinion factors will work to make unions more attractive to employees. One is the swing toward tax ceilings spearheaded by California's Proposition 13. Any shortage of tax dollars escalates political in-fighting for available funds, and at this, unions excel. Another factor is the wavering public attitude toward the cost benefits of higher education. Rising costs of a college education may cause young people to seek higher education over a longer period of time or to by-pass it entirely. Some states are limiting enrollments especially in high-cost programs. Coupled with fewer high school seniors during the eighties, these factors predict lower enrollments, fewer faculty positions, and the discontinuation of programs that fail to attract large numbers of students. The ensuing faculty rush for job security and benefits will certainly favor unionization in one form or another.

A trend toward the use of interest arbitration rather than strikes for settling negotiation deadlocks may reduce antiunion publicity. Unions traditionally have opposed arbitration because it ostensibly deprives them of their ultimate weapon, the strike. Strikes following arbitration almost always fail. Also employers generally abhor the right of a third party (arbiter) to determine how much of the budget must be spent on salaries and benefits. Growing public antipathy toward strikes, however, has led twenty-three states to make interest arbitration legal for fire fighters and police unions which, by the way, now seek a national law requiring arbitration. I believe that arbitration will almost completely replace the use of faculty strikes by the year 1990. Even liberal professors are, by and large, unwilling to strike for their own conditions of employment. Assured use of arbitration, a procedure more consistent with the principles of logic and reason that they teach, will make bargaining much more attractive to senior faculty members who have already achieved a measure of security.

Actions by College and University Executives and Trustees

During the sixties and seventies, college presidents and their assistants offered almost no realistic opposition to faculty bargaining. In fact, it was often their negative emotional responses to union organizers on campus that assured the growth of unionism. This careless type of response is rapidly being replaced by careful administrative planning and preparation. Salaries are more likely to be kept competitive with those at unionized campuses, faculty participation in academic and personnel decisions now generally receives administrative support, and judicial grievance procedures are replacing the old paternalistic mechanisms of never-ending administrative hearings. As stated earlier, unions along with affirmative-action rulings and court decisions can take much of the credit for these reforms, which in turn are fast becoming a significant obstacle to the spread of unions. In addition, universities are developing inhouse programs to educate administrators relative to the types of record keeping, personnel procedures, and grievance review that will avoid crises and improve faculty morale. And when a union election appears on the horizon, no effort will be spared in the future to see that trustees and administration are prepared to meet the situation calmly and to avoid the legal and personal entanglements that characterized and influenced so many faculty elections of the sixties and seventies.

Actions by Educational Unions

An interesting parallel exists among faculty unions. Just as college executives and trustees failed to organize a cooperative campaign to resist bargaining, the three major educational unions have been unable to achieve among themselves a first step toward peaceful coexistence and cooperation. Their internecine battles at campus elections created confusion and bitterness among faculty members whose trust and favorable votes were needed to make bargaining effective. Mutual distrust and pressures for immediate election victories caused unions to squander millions of dollars on competition, especially in New York and California. Similarly, at the national level, unions at every turn have undercut each other's political influence with Congress, and union disagreements almost lost the unusual opportunity to profit from White House support for a Department of Education. Some efforts at cooperation, and even merger, have surfaced from time to time, but by and large, they have been superficial causing more ill will than progress. New opportunities for membership expansion during the early eighties will encourage neither merger nor cooperation and, as a result, election campaigns and union services will continue to suffer until about 1990 when more serious attempts at interunion cooperation may hopefully emerge.

Actions by Labor-Relations Boards

Here again, faculty bargaining has not been given the help it needed. Too many members of state public-employment relations boards have been literally thrown into a maelstrom of labor wars without sufficient time, precedent, preparation, authority, or broad political support. Too often members were appointed on the basis of political loyalties rather than professional qualification. In fact, the legislation that created the boards seldom established professional standards of any kind, either for appointments to the board or for the judicial decisions to be rendered. A few laws in one manner or another tried to balance the biases of board appointments, but almost no attempt was made to limit appointments to experienced neutrals with a record of evenhanded, judicious decisions in similar or related work. Too many boards offered poor salaries and working conditions that could hardly be expected to attract and retain the level of leadership required to resolve labor disputes in a manner that would gain respect and build enduring case law. It took the Pennsylvania board five years of experience and an order by the state's highest court to begin to deal with the intricacies of scope in educational bargaining. This is not to blame members who had little experience or precedent in such matters and who were subjected to the worst kind of political pressures. Throughout the country most board members on first appointment not only were untrained and inexperienced in public-employee bargaining, they were naïve as to the nature of the higher education enterprise and its complicated mechanisms of self-governance. The net result was usually to place issues of faculty bargaining in the framework of industrial case law and precedent. It is difficult to assess the impact of this naïveté on the future of higher education. Certainly the traditional separation of public higher education from state politics has been all but destroyed, and it will be up to future historians to assess the effects. My criticism basically is directed at legislatures that, through careless labor legislation, destroyed important academic traditions in some states, violated education law in most states, established no substantial standards for labor boards, injected political agencies into academic affairs, and usually failed to recognize that they had done any of these things.[13] Whether or not states now considering legislation will do any better is pure conjecture.

The history of NLRB action in university bargaining is one generally marked by caution and trial and error. This is, by and large, to its credit because it indicates some recognition of differences existing between college governance and industrial management. After considerable vacillation in the early cases, especially in matters of unit determination, the Board's case-by-case decisions began to establish a set of detailed conditions, for example, for unit membership, that were carefully scrutinized prior to each new decision. This careful detailed approach is, on the whole, commendatory, and yet it poses problems. One obvious problem created by detail is that it offered each party the opportunity to raise detailed issue after issue, not so much for a fair unit determination as for a time delay that would be favorable to the party raising the issues. As an example, unions used delay tactics when they needed more time for recruiting votes prior to an election while management sought delays in order to push elections beyond the end of an academic year when faculty members who had been given notice of separation would no longer be eligible to vote. In other words, delays, as in the first election at New York University,[14] may have been more important than substantive issues in determining election outcomes. This is not news to the Board which is seeking remedies, but unfortunately time delay is only one of the prices that must be paid for excessive dependence on detail. Another outcome is that threat of future scrutiny by a labor board tends to force rigid application of detail on campuses prior to union elections. This may sound like, but not necessarily be, improved management. As an example, a campus facing future review has a tendency to spell out and publish a long list of detailed responsibilities and duties for department chairpersons to prove that they are indeed supervisors not eligible under labor law for future union membership. Unfortunately, the next step is to force each chairperson to execute each detail faithfully and to make records, usually written memoranda, to provide substantive evidence for future hearings. As good as this may sound to business-oriented thinkers, it is not the method preferred by academics since it tends to overmechanize decisions that may more effectively be accomplished by consensus among professionals. The search for hard, indisputable evidence upon which to evaluate teaching performance, as an example, can result in simplistic rather than sophisticated standards and procedures, too easily met by people of lesser credentials. It also tends to create ill will among colleagues. An example is the effect that detail may have on the handling of ordinary discipline problems. Where a person-to-person confidential discussion of a faculty member's shortcoming had been generally effective, deans and chairpersons under the pressures of accumulating evidence for future hearings (or formal grievances) feel obliged to write memoranda to record evidence of their disciplinary actions. Disciplinary memoranda have a way of starting a paper war and creating fears and ill will of a lasting character. So it is that labor boards, by using detailed examination of management practices in unit hearings, can create pressures toward mechanical managerial uniformity that may be injurious to the personalized character and quality of higher education. Labor boards and legislative committees have as yet no way of experiencing or reviewing these effects. Interestingly enough, when labor boards accede to union wishes by designating department chairpersons as members of the union, departmental decisions are almost always subjected to closer administrative review at higher levels, which means that the decision-making process moves away from the localized departmental concensus (which faculty members cherish) to a more hierarchical determination. Thus labor-board methods, as well as decisions, can have a direct effect on the management structures of universities, making them appear and act more like business and industrial organizations. The net results, good and bad, are impossible to evaluate accurately. Yet it is clear that labor boards have a responsibility for knowing a great deal more about the purposes and character of the higher education enterprise, which in a sense they now partially supervise.

A more obvious impact is generated by labor-board decisions relative to the scope of faculty bargaining. To date, NLRB and its regional officers have been conservative in delimiting the scope of faculty bargaining probably because industrial case law was rather strictly applied to higher education. This procedure, however, may change as faculty unions continue to press for a broader interpretation of "conditions of employment" that will permit more faculty influence on a wider range of management decisions. As more private college faculties seek the right to bargain, some appropriate agency such as the Brookings Institution or The Academic Collective Bargaining Information Service, might well be funded to investigate the long-range impact of labor-board decisions not only on academic labor relations but on the structure and character of the educational enterprise.

Call for Leadership

Collective bargaining is usually established not as an end in itself, but as a means to transcendent purpose. Congress wrote into the NLRA that it shall be "the policy of the United States to eliminate the causes of certain substantial obstructions to the free flow of commerce...." Evidently its intent was that collective bargaining was to serve the larger purpose of increasing the free flow of commerce. The New York State Legislature stated that the purpose of its Taylor Law was "to promote harmonious and cooperative relationships... and to assure... the orderly and uninterrupted operations and functions of government....." The object of the law as applied to the State University of New York appears to be the achievement of cooperation and harmony among the parties and to provide continuous educational services. (Parenthetically, it is interesting to note that the legislature must have thought it could better achieve harmony and cooperation by taking the administrative function of bargaining away from the chancellor and trustees and assigning it to an office of employee relations that had no experience with, and little understanding of, university governance.) These larger goals of cooperation and service then are the ongoing responsiblity of both parties. But I foresee little progress toward these goals during the eighties. Unions will still be competing for new membership in states passing new enabling legislation. College and university presidents will still find solace in decrying, but doing little about, the negative aspects of faculty unions and senates. Labor boards will still be underfunded and undermanned. I would guess that 1990-1995 would be the earliest period when the public might expect a change in conditions that will encourage serious consideration of cooperation and joint leadership toward goals of public service in addition to the usual goals of self-service.

Currently each national and state educational union expends much of its resources in promoting legislation, campus organization, training programs, and biased publicity about its latest achievements. By 1995 there will be few states without laws on the books (although amendments will be needed), there will be fewer aggrieved faculties worth the effort and price to organize, and, it is hoped, more of the publicity will be directed toward future possibilities and advantages of merger and cooperation among unions. This happy prediction, of course, will depend on mutual trust among union leaders, which may not be possible until new leadership emerges. Merger or strong affiliation among national unions is a step necessary to reduce costs and achieve a measure of internal union security. Out of affiliation will come agreements and a more united front relative to future legislation, campus elections, and joint efforts at providing publicity and services to the members generally. This interunion cooperation and security must be achieved before unions will consider cooperation with university management toward broad social ends intended by legislation.

Similarly, college and university presidents by 1990 will be much more accustomed to and much less insecure about unions. Sooner or later they will discover the fact that faculty senates have become more like unions and unions have become more like faculty senates. Antiunion discussions will subside and the usual issues of money, institutional quality, and government regulations will again be the most pressing agenda at administrators' conferences. By 1990 there will be many examples of universities where administrators and faculty unions have pooled their political and manpower resources to improve university funding. It happens occasionally in 1980, but cooperation is more by coincidence than by design. In fact, politicians at the bargaining table today would probably resent a double-barrelled assault by the academy whereby management helps unions in seeking more money for faculty compensation, and unions bargain funds for broad institutional purposes. But this also will be not uncommon strategy by 1990, and it should lay the groundwork for cooperation in the search for institutional excellence.

It will be extremely difficult for unions and university presidents to end their current efforts at mutual destruction. Unions have prospered by rallying faculty members against what they considered to be arbitrary and capricious actions of authoritarian administrators. And it is difficult to change a winning game. Yet by 1990 unions should be feeling increased difficulties in trying to capitalize on faculty-administration problems that have been steadily eased over two decades of bargaining and affirmative action. Then educational unions may feel pressures to seek a new approach. When this happens, unions will discover that administrators can be helpful allies in union effectiveness.

Currently university officials severely criticize faculty unions as enemies of educational quality. Specifically they blame unions for (1) protecting incompetents, (2) processing petty grievances, (3) impeding educational change, (4) lowering academic standards for faculty promotion and tenure, (5) decreasing the amount of faculty and administrator time available for academic matters, and (6) attacking administrators falsely to serve union ends. I predict that as administrators learn how to work with union leaders during the eighties, they will find union channels at least as timely and responsive as the usual faculty senate, and more decisive. By 1990 unions will find it less rewarding to attack administrators, and most grievances will be processed routinely and with little publicity. Petty grievances will receive summary attention because they will have become more of a nuisance to unions than to administrators. Almost no one will be talking about the cost of unions except the members. And it is entirely possible and likely that union leadership will be passed along in the eighties to less strident faculty voices interested in institutional vitality as a means of job security. Should these predictions come true, union attitudes will be more supportive of high academic standards, and faculty committees will ordinarily refuse to recommend tenure or promotion for an incompetent regardless of a procedural lapse by some administrative office. I am not saying that at some future time there will be no conflicting interests between the parties. Such a state of bliss is not only not possible, but infeasible. Faculty members will always be protective of the status quo, at least in their own departments, and administration will always be pushing for changes, not all of which will be for the better. It is this difference in perception along with a balance of power that generates vitality without loss of stability in academic governance. What I am suggesting is that most future conflicts will be moved through channels as normal items of daily business clearing the way for the parties to see common goals and problems. Negotiating conditions of employment certainly should not prevent the parties legally or emotionally from combining their intellect and influence to solve institutional problems beyond the bargaining table. Perhaps the university's most glaring weakness in a highly politicized society is its inability to protect itself adequately against the powerful self-interest groups that lobby daily in the nation's capital. Higher education lobbies are woefully weak for a variety of reasons. Yet a combination of these institutional associations working closely with national faculty unions could provide the type of political clout needed in the years ahead. As an example, the tax-exempt status of private colleges and educational foundations is being challenged more sharply each time someone puts it on the national agenda. Bureaucratic interpretations of law and the resulting arbitrary and capricious regulations need more challenge than can be provided by logic and reason alone. Since 1960 private colleges and universities have become almost as dependent as public institutions upon state and federal appropriations. Surely these and other issues go beyond the bargaining table in requiring the unified attention and efforts of faculty, administration, and trustees.

As enrollments decrease in the eighties, governments will question the need for a plethora of colleges and universities both private and public. Legislators, regardless of personal loyalties to one or another institution, are not likely to find it politically feasible to close or severely cut back public institutions. Many private institutions will depend more and more on political effectiveness for survival. This alone may make union affiliation more attractive to faculties and administrators at private colleges. These thoughts are, I realize, repugnant to many people on each side of the fence, but it is not too early to set aside some of our prejudices in order to at least think about the realities that are shaping the future of higher education.

In conclusion, it is my conviction that mature faculty unions of the nineties will look and act like long-established faculty senates and that, to their own surprise, many college presidents will accept union presence as a normal collegial-type operation. This change will occur at public institutions more readily than at private ones. Not until the nineties will private-college administrators and faculties begin to view faculty unionization as an instrument of institutional excellence and survival. If and when these changes in perception occur, they will be accompanied by fundamental alterations in governance structures, not the least of which will be faculty representation on boards of trustees. In a sense, I see faculty unionization as a natural process by which faculties not enfranchised by charter, achieve recognition and collegium through civil processes. Once achieved, educators will no longer be interested in questioning the validity of unions in the profession of education; rather, they will be debating the proper use of educational-political power in shaping public policy beyond academic borders.

Notes

1. Morris Bishop, *A History of Cornell* (Ithaca, N.Y.: Cornell University Press, 1962), p. 264.
2. Examples are Kent State University and the five universities under the jurisdiction of the Illinois Board of Governors.
3. *U.S. News and World Report*, October 22, 1979, p. 69.
4. *Special Report No. 12*, Academic Collective Bargaining Information Service: Washington, D.C., 1980.

5. *U.S. News and World Report*, December 10, 1979, p. 96.

6. Jamestown College, North Dakota, and New England College, New Hampshire.

7. Central Michigan University and the State University of New York.

8. See G.W. Angell and E.P. Kelley, *Faculty Bargaining under Trustee Policy*, Monograph 7 (Washington, D.C.: Academic Collective Bargaining Information Service, Project on Educational Employment Relations, 1979).

9. For a more complete discussion, see *Special Report 29*, "Management Prerogatives and Faculty Rights" (Washington, D.C.: Academic Collective Bargaining Information Service, 1977).

10. *National League of Cities* v. *Usery*, 96 S. Ct. 2465 (1976).

11. *NLRB and the Yeshiva University Faculty Association v. Yeshiva University*, 582 F. 2d 686 (1978).

12. *U.S. News and World Report*, October 22, 1979, p. 69.

13. See my essay on the subject, *Legislatures, Collective Bargaining and the Public University*, Monograph 4 (Washington, D.C.: Academic Collective Bargaining Information Service, 1977).

14. See Gerald Bodner, *The "No Agent" Vote at N.Y.U.: A Concise Legal History,* Special Report 9 (Washington, D.C.: Academic Collective Bargaining Information Service, 1974).

2

Commentary

Woodley B. Osborne

In chapter 1, Angell makes a number of points with which I wholeheartedly agree. Like Angell, I believe that faculty unions have been and can continue to be a positive force in higher education. But I disagree with what I take to be one of Angell's central premises: "The debate as to the validity of unionism on campus is for all intents and purposes over." Despite the fact that formal faculty collective bargaining has now been around for a substantial period of time and despite the fact that it is doubtless accepted as the norm on many campuses, there persists across academe an ambivalence not only toward faculty collective bargaining but, more broadly, toward the overall relationship of faculty to administration and governing board. In my judgment, one cannot adequately assess the results of faculty collective bargaining or gauge its future growth without keeping this ambivalence—and the debate it has engendered—firmly in mind.

This debate over faculty unionism had until recently lagged somewhat in intensity. It has now been revived by the Supreme Court's resolution of the *Yeshiva* case. Though there is much one can say about the *Yeshiva* decision, it suffices to say here that the Court's effort has yielded the same inconclusive, divided and generally unsatisfactory results that have characterized earlier and less magisterial versions of the controversy. One does not have to read Justice Powell's majority decision very closely to discern his view that collective bargaining has little or no place on the campus. Nor is it hard to tell that Justice Brennan, writing for the minority, holds an opposite view from Powell's on the merits of faculty collective bargaining as well as on the legal issue that confronted the Court.

What is interesting about the *Yeshiva* decision for my limited purposes is the extent to which it mirrors academe's own ambivalence. At issue in *Yeshiva* was the question of whether or not the Yeshiva faculty were "managerial employees" and as such not entitled to bargain with the protection of the National Labor Relations Act. More than anything else, managerial status in this sense depends on an "alignment with management." Powell concluded that the reliance of the Yeshiva administration and governing board on faculty recommendations in a variety of areas of importance to the institutional mission was more than enough to establish this alignment.

The labor board's general counsel and the Yeshiva University Faculty Association both argued that the reliance on faculty recommendations was simply a by-product of the faculty's professionalism and stressed as well that the faculty was entirely independent of any "managerial" control when it made these recommendations. Justice Powell largely agreed. He concluded, however, that these factors simply bolstered his ultimate conclusion that the faculty interests and those of Yeshiva administration governing board were aligned because they showed the extent and the necessity of institutional reliance on faculty advice. Justice Brennan, by contrast, accused Powell of viewing academic governance "through a rose-colored lens," thereby obscuring his perception of the more or less hierarchical structure that had long since displaced the collegium.

As most honest observers of the scene would admit, there is truth in both of these apparently incompatible conclusions. That is why the ambivalence and the debate and the confusion about faculty collective bargaining persist. I would argue that Justice Brennan was the more correct; and that, in any event, Justice Powell's conclusions do not support the legal result he reached, either as a matter of law or of policy. But the point here is simply that while it is true that many private four-year and graduate institutions are increasingly run by a largely antonomous administration, it is also true that at many of these same institutions, the faculty play an undeniably important role in decision making in a number of areas.

From the beginning, the debate over faculty collective bargaining has been between those who emphasize one or the other of the foregoing factors— frequently to the exclusion of the other. And that, to my mind, is one of the reasons the confusion persists. For in my judgment it is only when one recognizes the presence of *both* an active and independent administration *and* a legitimate and important faculty role that one can properly assess the real or potential impact of collective bargaining. Similarly, in gauging the likely spread of collective bargaining, one simply must keep in mind the extent to which many in the professoriate believe that the proper faculty role in governance can be established only by consent; and that any attempt to establish or preserve traditional faculty influence through formal collective bargaining is inevitably self-defeating.

I believe Angell has paid too little attention to these considerations in his otherwise excellent and informative piece. Accordingly, in the brief space remaining, I would like to elaborate my views regarding the impact of this "industrywide ambivalence." It is necessary, of course, for purposes of this brief analysis, to separate the public from the private sector. Both the reasons for engaging in collective bargaining and its results differ markedly between the two sectors. I shall discuss the public sector first.

In the public sector this ambivalence has not retarded the growth of faculty collective bargaining to the extent it has in the private sector. In the public sector the relationship between faculty and administration and governing board, while obviously still important, is only part of the problem, given the financial dependence on the state legislature and the managerial role played by the executive branch of states like New York. No one can dispute, in these circumstances, the need for an effective relationship between institution and state government. And even those inclined toward the most altruistic view of collegiality or shared authority have tended to agree that it is imperative that the faculty voice be expressed clearly and separately from that of an institution's administration and governing board. It is simply too much to expect the faculty viewpoint—acknowledgedly critical to the success of the institution—to be expressed other than by the faculty itself. The relative consensus on this point—entirely lacking in the private sector—accounts for the much more rapid spread of faculty collective bargaining in the public sector than in the private. I believe that this disparity in growth will continue.

With regard to the success of faculty unions in the public sector, I would make one or two simple observations. The more successful public-sector faculty unions have concentrated on establishing a good and effective relationship with the state government, understanding that this is why they got elected in the first place. Accomplishing this concentration, however, has been far from easy. This is so for a number of reasons, but principally because most state labor laws require the faculty to bargain with their administrations or governing boards and acknowledge no direct role between union and legislature or executive branch. Accordingly, in the early years of such bargaining relationships, a faculty union's attention must focus on establishing the basic agreement with its governing board. Thereafter, however, the relationship with the state government, critical to the success and ongoing utility of the union, must be addressed. In my judgment, a close look at the evidence will show that the successful faculty unions have done this; while the less successful ones have not for whatever reason.

The private sector is another matter entirely. I have long since given up arguing that collegiality and/or shared authority are not necessarily incompatible with collective bargaining. However true that may be in the abstract, it becomes true in practice only when a majority of the faculty at a given institution either believe it to be so or have so despaired of collegiality as to be willing to displace it with something more vigorous. That these majorities are rather slow in forming is confirmed by the relatively small number of formally organized faculties in the private sector. Still, that growth, while slow, also appears to be sure. I believe it will continue at essentially the current rate.

In assessing the results of faculty collective bargaining in the private sector, the primary inquiry should be whether or not the faculty role in governance has been effectively diminished through collective bargaining. While this emphasis may seem odd, it is, I believe, correct. There is no reason—in theory or in practice—that faculty unions in the private sector may not enjoy reasonable success in the bread-and-butter issues that preoccupy most unions: compensation, job security, and effective grievance procedures. Angell argues that they can and have achieved such success—at least in reasonable measure—and my observation confirms this. But this conclusion does not address academe's overriding concerns about collective bargaining. As I have indicated, controversy and doubt remain because of the persistent view that collective bargaining can only damage the traditional faculty role in governance and that this damage is not worth the gains the union may achieve. For that reason, I believe the most useful inquiry—and also the most difficult—remains.

3

Commentary

Anthony V. Sinicropi

George Angell has indeed developed a thorough and thought-provoking paper, which in my estimation has dealt with the campus collective-bargaining phenomenon in a most comprehensive, yet succinct, manner. In general, I am in accord with his reportings and prognostications. When I do find any reason for differences, it is usually a matter of degree or emphasis rather than outright dispute.

Roots of Faculty Bargaining

While he has developed a number of major themes, the overriding one that has struck me is the thesis that union roots in the academic setting began, at least philosophically, with faculty bodies such as faculty senates; and in the not-too-distant future, faculty unions, which will be representing nearly 90 percent of all college and university faculties, will again behave and resemble those faculty-senate groups. I endorse the latter part of this theme, but I do not find any basis to conclude that faculty-senate groups carried on any kind of collective-bargaining function or gave rise to faculty unions as we know them in present times. If there is any validity to the argument that faculty-senate bodies were the forerunners of faculty unions, the appropriate analogy would be that company unions were the progenitors of legitimate labor unions in America. While I do not believe faculty senates were management-inspired institutions developed to fend off unions, I do believe the operation and composition of faculty-senate groups were for the purposes of assisting management or administration in discharging its responsibilities. That is not nor has it ever been the function of unions except in those rare instances where unions become the more powerful member of the bilateral relationship, and management depended on the union for its very existence.

Editor's Note: The remarks in this section have been prepared with four objectives in mind. They address chapter 1 by Angell and offer a reaction thereto; they voice my own statements that may be nothing more than embellishments of Angell's thoughts or, at times, differences with his views; they offer my perspective as one who has been a teacher-scholar and later an administrator in both the small liberal-arts-college setting and later, in the major state university environment for nearly a quarter century; and they are my observations as a practicing professional neutral who has mediated and arbitrated higher education disputes for over a decade. Admittedly, these four objectives are not without influence on one another, and they will often collide. Nevertheless, my task and my background make up the biases and the resultant product.

A close look at faculty-senate groups reveals that they are usually made up of the most respected and accomplished faculty or those faculty who possess the most promising potential. As such, they do not necessarily reflect the desires and wishes of their less fortunate colleagues. In addition, they most often direct their activities toward educational policy matters and make recommendations to administrators. In this regard, they have an ideological or philosophical orientation, and such a posture is antithetical to American trade-union behavior, even as they have evolved and developed in the academic area. While there are several points to be made here, the one that I am most concerned with is that unions behave differently than faculty-senate bodies, past and present, and I cannot find any activities of consequence in the past development of faculty-senate bodies that has given rise to faculty unions.

As for the future, I do agree that faculty unions may very well begin behaving as other faculty bodies have. This conclusion is predicated on the internal and external developments that affect the union and college administrators' associations. As resources become scarce for colleges, as student numbers decline, as faculty benefits suffer, as society alters its priorities away from educational institutions (if that be the case), the problem confronting the two groups, unions and college administration, are of mutual concern and thus the parties may assume a more accommodative mutual solving posture. It is no secret that union-management relationships often evolve through a series of stages: hostility and open conflict to acceptance and accommodation to cooperation and mutual problem solving. The dialectic may be equally applicable to the campus-bargaining situation, particularly when problems of mutual concern confront the parties. Moreover, when principals and personalities change and maturity develops, the more logical and philosophical approach to bargaining relationship prevails. Thus it is not unreasonable to expect that faculty unions of the future will resemble faculty-senate bodies, both in structure, operation, and substantive concern.

Current Status of Unions

I wholeheartedly concur with the assessment and predictions on union development and growth in higher education. The trends have been consistent and I do not foresee any factors that act to moderate these trends. There is one proviso, however, and I shall address that concern in a later section.

Success of Faculty Unions

In examining Angell's six criteria for determining union success, again I am in general accord except for sometimes having different reasons for arriving at the same conclusions. His explanation of faculty-union behavior on economic matters is purely predictable. Unions, as self-interest groups, must compete against rival unions, that is, other faculty unions on the same or other campuses or unions representing other on-campus employees, and therefore it is predictable for them to seek to have new priorities for resources as opposed to looking for greater institutional appropriations. In that same connection, it must be observed that faculty unions embrace the general philosophy of American unionism, espouse a nonphilosophical or pragmatic approach. American unions are nonideological and faculty unions are not an exception to this rule. One should bear in mind, however, that as resources become less available and the competition becomes more keen, the unions in the public sector have not been above going the political route to alter this trend. In that sense, public unions, including faculty organizations, cease being nonpolitical, yet remain nonideological. The problem with this approach is that it distorts collective bargaining, at least as we know it in the United States; it is being carried on at one level, between the parties, and it is simultaneously being pursued at a higher plane such as governing board, legislative, or gubernatorial level. Angell referred to this by pointing out that the unions in such situations may become too powerful and influential. That, indeed, is a concern, but an equally disturbing factor is what this condition does to the decision-making apparatus of the academic institution. Elevating bargaining above the level of local unit administrators threatens to take the decision-making function away from the institutional decision maker and elevates it to a political body. That fact may cause a centralization of decision making, and faculty unionization that pursues the bargaining with this dual-level approach accomplishes something that even faculty do not seek. It removes from the faculty and local administrators the control of the educational program since fiscal and resource-allocation decisions are being determined at the political level. The danger of this bilevel bargaining development is the potential wresting of educational policy decisions from educators and placing it into the hands of politicians and/or influential alumni or government-board members. This indeed would be a severe loss to education.

The irony of this possible development is that in the long run unions have not been found to have been responsible for changing the salary or wage level of organized employees. Angell has correctly related that initially unions do increase wages or salaries or they may even cause a compression effect on salary structures, but over the long haul the market, even with its inefficiencies, is the real determinant of compensation systems. It is indeed alarming that university and college faculties do not comprehend this fact and are willing to jeopardize their own influence on curriculum and educational policy in pursuit of an imaginary monetary gain goal through bargaining.

I agree that personnel policies tend to become more predictable from the faculty members' perspective as a result of bargaining. However, there is no evidence that bargained procedures are more equitable. To be sure, promotion and tenure as well as merit salary decisions made in the absence of a bargaining model may be thought of as capricious or arbitrary by many faculty, but that assessment is not necessarily correct regarding the fairness or equity of such decision. In the absence of bargaining, the tenure and promotion decisions are the result of both faculty and administration input, and the criteria are often more rigorous in this setting than in the bargaining posture. Thus the bargaining model may well accommodate a faulty perception of fairness but also may contribute toward a dimension of standards.

Even if bargaining inserts itself in the tenure-promotion decision, there is no real indication the results will be severely altered. For example, as an arbitrator, I have often been asked to decide if a promotion were procedurally and substantively fair. In almost all instances, the decision by the administrators made with faculty input have prevailed. Even if I would have made a different decision, the key to a proper determination is not whether a different result should occur but whether the assessment was done fairly and under the procedures and determined on the basis of agreed-upon criteria. Only if the procedure were violated could a decision be set aside, and then the usual remedy would be to reorder the evaluation so that it was conducted in a non-discriminatory manner.

As for salary, the bargaining arena tends to destroy the merit system of rewards and often encourage the use of pay-scheduled plans. While this system is not necessarily evil, it does tend to curtail the flexibility of rewards.

What comes to mind is that bargaining tends to intrude on the flexibility of the administration's decision-making apparatus and tends to structure the system. This consequence not only curtails administrative flexibility but also rigidifies behavior, duties, and responsibilities. While decisions may appear to be more even-handed and equitable, and are more predictable, the codification and structuring of these decisions mitigates against the kind of freedom that has long been associated with the academic environment. To put it another way, equitable treatment does not necessarily mean equal treatment, and bargaining usually attempts to secure equal treatment. It tends to have a leveling influence that accommodates most people in a work setting but often at the expense of those few who excel. That goal is commendable and even necessary in most work settings, but in my judgment, it is not a desired objective in the academic world of higher education.

This same analysis applies to Angell's fourth criterion. Standardization of workloads, assignment of research assistants, and so on, tends to develop under bargaining. But again all faculty members do not utilize their time in the same manner, nor should they. Some are better teachers, and others are better researchers. There is no such thing as an "average" faculty member. Thus, while bargaining may certainly equalize the availability and use of resources, this result is not necessarily desirable. I do agree that differentiation among colleges on a campus might allow for some flexibility, but this does little for the structural result within a college. Perhaps one example will highlight my concern. A senior faculty member might be a well-recognized and well-rewarded scholar-teacher. He or she then takes on a young colleague as a protegé, and in such a relationship the elder faculty member offers guidance to the younger one with respect to research thrust and even agrees to a heavier teaching load *vis-à-vis* research programs to allow the younger member to have more time for research and thus achieve promotion and proper recognition as well as more development. It is difficult for this relationship to exist when bargaining establishes a uniform allocation for teaching and research loads, graduate-student supervision, utilization of research assistants, course, course choices, grants, and so on.

I do believe that the introduction of a grievance-arbitration procedure for redress of alleged violated rights is indeed a positive and perhaps the most important contribution of faculty unionism. Presently faculty have appeals procedures for alleged wrongs committed against them, but in the absence of faculty unionism, the final arbiter of their alleged wrong is the administration. While those of us in the academic community respect the fairness of college administrators, their biases sometimes crop up to occlude their vision in the disposition of these matters. In addition, the faculties' perception of fair treatment by an outside arbiter of an unbiased nature is important.

As for greater direct contact between faculty and college administrators, I do not see collective bargaining as a vehicle for improving this condition. Even if such contact becomes greater, it is often in an adversarial setting and thus the bargaining structure does little to enhance the collegial posture so essential in academia.

In sum, I believe that unions indeed have been successful in achieving the six goals and objectives as outlined by Angell, but I do not believe the attainment of several of the goals makes for a better educational environment for faculty or for administrator.

Other Effects of Faculty Bargaining

The less tangible effects of unionization on the campus are indeed as important as those that are more concretely defined and recognized. Four major elements were treated in the segment: (1) effect on other campuses and the administration policies; (2) political involvement; (3) redefinition of governing-board behavior; and (4) cost of educational services. In a sense, these topics have already been addressed; however, there are some loose ends that need attending.

Effect on Other Campuses

Several years ago Arthur Ross defined trade-union behavior by stressing their political nature. That is, if viewed as an economic institution, a union is difficult to understand. But if union decision making is analyzed in the context of its being a political institution, its behavior is rational. One of the factors that influences bargaining posture is the benefits realized by other unions in the same industry or by competing bargaining units. Ross called this phenomenon "orbits of coercive comparison"—the union will seek to receive benefits similar to those realized by competing groups. That expectancy is not unreasonable, and likewise it is reasonable to expect that most organized institutions will grant benefits to its employees similar to those organized by a union. In that regard a unionized campus will impose itself on nonorganized campuses. However, as stated earlier, that effect will be felt only in the short run because over time the benefit level will be determined by market forces rather than the degree of unionization. This is readily apparent if one looks at wage structures in unionized and nonunionized industries generally. The fact that unions have been most successful in better-paying industries should not be construed to mean that unions have been responsible for those higher wages. The economics of the industry more often dictates the wage and benefit level. The same will be true in education.

As for its effect on management, there is no question that the presence of a union will make it more efficient. Academic management was never accused of being efficient. However, it was not designed with that purpose in mind. It was set up to coordinate the desires and needs of the faculty. In that sense it was there to serve the faculty. However, as we moved from an elitist educational society to one favoring higher education for the masses and as we altered the focus of higher education from small liberal-arts colleges to major state institutions with massive state and federal aid and with more emphasis on specialized-skill training (as well as education), the need for more professional management arose. Concurrent with the rise of that bureaucracy, more rules requirements were needed. The professional administrators were thus confronted with controls on their flexible decision-making authority. The rise of unionization and its contract requirements have yet added another restrictive control on the administrator's decision-making flexibility. Given these developments, university administrators have been suspicious, critical, and even fearful of unions. Perhaps as new managers come onto the scene, their posture will be altered. Nevertheless, their ability to lead has been constrained.

The just described development has caused educational administrators to become specialized to the extent that educational and professional administrative leaders are now vying for the authority to lead the institutions. Academic leaders are not prepared to deal with these intrusions on the academic directions they seek to pursue. However, absent the complement of professional administrators, they (the academic leaders) are at a loss to move the educational institutions toward the academic goals because of bureaucratic and union intrusion. In my view, the collective-bargaining condition has caused a leadership crisis on campus, and it is not clear which group shall prevail, the educators or the professionals. My best guess is that the professionals are becoming more powerful and influential.

Again, a case study might be instructive. In current times students are leaving liberal-arts areas and are crowding into career and vocationally oriented colleges—or units on major campuses. If resources are not proportionally allocated to meet these student ebbs and flows to and from liberal education and professional schools, then disparate workloads between faculty occur. This teeter-totter has been the case of universities for years. However, given enough time and a cyclical pattern, a return to normalcy in workload occurs. But with unionization and the quest for equality of treatment, the possibility of faculty redistribution becomes a reality. Given that state of affairs, tenure becomes an expendable item, and the educational direction of the institution becomes a result of the market as opposed to desires of the educators. In my judgment, unionization will accentuate this change, and professional managers will be more willing to meet this challenge by altering the faculty complement than an academic leader would. These kinds of decisions may very well be politically popular and might even be encouraged by the union but may well have a detrimental effect on the quality of the education.

Along with such changes will be cost increases. Already academic top administrative levels have been broadened by the needs to comply with the myriad laws and regulations. The union as a new kid on the block will only increase the level of administration's needs.

Keys to the Future

Unquestionably legislation and the courts have not stilled the march of unionization. While the *Yeshiva* decision may very well stem the tide of union development among private schools, I view this decision as an anomoly. While there may be many reasons to turn unionism aside on the college campus, I do not believe the courts' rationale in that decision constitutes a logical ground to that end.

Some General Thoughts on the Topic

Faculties have always had a good deal to say about how and what a university is about. That is as it should be! Strong faculties tend to have more to say about educational matters than do weak ones. And that is as it should be! However, it seems to me that unionization has made its inroads in the academic setting where faculties have not been strong in determining educational policy or because the faculties, even though academically strong, have been deprived the resources because political decisions by governing boards or politicians have divested them of the decision-making power regarding academic matters through the control of fiscal matters. In either situation it is only logical to conclude that the faculty will seek to restore its control and have often done so through unionization. As resources continue to be difficult to come by, the unionization of the college campuses will continue, no matter what the strength of the faculty.

Accompanying this change, however, will come a gradual erosion of university and college administrators' decision-making authority. I see more professional management where decisions will be based on market conditions such as student demands for career choices and political exigencies. With increasing technology and the need for technicians in society, there will be a decline in liberal-arts programs and a rise of professional and career programs. Unions will tend to seek uniformity of treatment for faculty, and this quest for equality will put a substantial burden on administrators. These developments may seriously alter the character of university faculties.

Presently faculty loyalties are first to their discipline and then to the institution. If the constraints become as great as they appear in the predictions, faculty loyalties may very well shift to the institution because of the unionized protections. Only those few superstars with impeccable credentials will be able to retain loyalties to the discipline as opposed by the institution. Alternatively, as unions develop it is possible that a type of craft unionism could occur on each campus where faculties will retain disciplinary loyalties but through union affiliation.

While these predictions seem dire there are some alternatives that may conceivably alter the course of events. In contemporary America, unions are not held in high esteem. More important than the popular notion of unions is the attitude of American business toward unions. When unions were less democratic and were guided by benevolent leaders such as John L. Lewis and Walter Reuther, management could depend on the bargain struck with such men. But as union membership became more militant and as the unions became more democratic, they became less predictable in their behavior. Given that condition, business has become less inclined to accept unions as a convenient appendage to their business. Faculty unions are perhaps even more democratic in their behavior than their industrial counterparts. If the degree of unpredictability is beyond the ability of university administrators to effectively deal with it, then they too may seek to find a method to operate in "union-free environment." Should that attitude prevail, unionism on the campus could fade.

I agree that what is needed is a strong leadership cadre in America's institutions of higher education. They must be attuned to educational needs of society, but likewise they should be prepared to critically examine the faculty's role on the campus. The collegium in the traditional sense and the isolated medieval university is no longer the prevailing condition. Whether unions develop and grow or whether they wither away, the leadership must lead and be prepared to make the right decisions. Finally, the new college leader must be a professional who has the proper knowledge of educational priorities, or a dedicated educator who has acquired professional management skills. Likewise, the union leader in higher education and the faculties must be aware of the costs of unionization as well as the benefits.

4 Commentary

Robert D. Helsby

As a young government administrator, one of the most significant learning experiences I had occurred while serving as an executive officer under Dr. Martin P. Catherwood, former dean of the School of Industrial and Labor Relations at Cornell University and at that time, industrial commissioner of the State of New York. One of his favorite teaching techniques was to present me with a long, bureaucratic or academic study, instructing me to tell him what it said in one page. While any such attempt to capsulize chapter 1 is certainly not easy—and indeed it might prove downright disastrous—I believe that summarizing it will be of great help in providing some structure to my own commentary.

Chapter 1 represents a balanced assessment of the advent of collective bargaining to higher education in these first twenty years of its existence. I say "balanced" because it is presented by a scholar of the subject who has personally experienced all aspects of the equation—teacher, professor, administrator, neutral, and researcher. More important, Angell was a college administrator who experienced the beginning traumas of the change from a relatively traditional system of collegiality and governance to the establishment of faculty unions on his campus.

Chapter 1 deals with the following four major aspects of collective bargaining in higher education:

1. The genesis and the current and future status of collective bargaining in higher education.
2. A look at the collective-bargaining process and its acceptance on campus.
3. An assessment of the success of collective bargaining and its effects on higher education.
4. What lies ahead as higher education faces the last two decades of the century and attempts to accommodate the bargaining process.

I will comment on each of these ideas and add some thoughts of my own.

The Genesis and the Current and Future Status of Collective Bargaining in Higher Education

I can find little argument with the factual documentation concerning the advent of collective bargaining in higher education. The facts are there, and there is no need to repeat them. The reasons for this veritable explosion, however, deserve comment.

When all the camouflage has been cleared away, collective bargaining is a shared-management process in one specialized area of management decision-making—the conditions of employment for employees. One might have expected that higher education would have reacted and adapted to the collective-bargaining process with facility and ease. After all, higher education has taken pride over the centuries in the principle that the academic faculty share in the administrative or management process—a process that has become known in higher education circles as collegiality and governance. One could well have reasoned that the extension of this principle to faculty participation in determining the nitty gritty of conditions under which they work would have been a relatively simple and easy process. Not so.

Higher education has tended to view with concern and alarm the possibility of unionization and the entrance of collective bargaining to the higher education domain. I have heard some of our nation's most distinguished educators stand before audiences and claim that the entrée of collective bargaining into higher education would destroy the university. Such contentions are almost reminiscent of the late thirties when the Wagner Act was passed and when the prime contention of business management was that collective bargaining would destroy the decision-making power of management and thus would become the tool of its employees. That notion, while not totally obsolete, is rarely heard now after more than forty years with the collective-bargaining process in the private sector.

In many colleges and universities, governance has long produced heavy faculty involvement and in many instances, control of such elements as faculty hiring, promotion, discharge, and discipline. In a number of the prestigious colleges and universities, governance invaded some of the so-called sacred management rights of the private sector such as selection and hiring of management personnel, and decisions on policy that run the gamut from curriculum to faculty freedom of speech.

When New York's Taylor Law was passed in 1967, if someone had asked me whether I thought that higher education should be covered under the law, I suspect I would have advised against it. I would have done so on the grounds that nobody really knew enough about collective bargaining in the public sector, let alone in the very unique area of higher education, to establish any systematic directions with confidence. There is still a great deal of discussion about the issue of whether collective bargaining really belongs in higher education and if it does, what type of collective bargaining.

I totally agree with Angell's statement that "larger forces of tradition and social changes may be worthy of more attention than heretofore given as causes of the upswing in faculty bargaining during the late sixties and seventies.

This change in society is a bit like the analogy I heard on the floor of the New York Legislature some time ago when a senator said, "It doesn't do me a bit of good to argue against the Rocky Mountains. The fact is they exist." Likewise, the right for citizens in a free and open society to inject their views into the decisions that vitally affect them exists. It is clear that the negotiating society is here to stay.

Collective bargaining is the response to a basic change in society. It has emerged as a process in which many differing positions can be brought together at the bargaining table, discussed openly, decided jointly, and recorded permanently in a collective-bargaining agreement. In its best form, it substitutes persuasion and reason for muscle and clout. Angell summarized this position as follows:

> Thus I see faculty bargaining as an integral part of the historical movement toward collegial management of academic affairs.

Whether any individual likes it or not, the negotiating society has become a way of life, and the better part of valor is to learn the process and to determine what makes the best sense in adapting it to higher education.

I also concur with Angell's position regarding the outlook for collective bargaining in higher education. In addition to the twenty-four states already permitting faculty bargaining, the process is actually taking place in many other states without the official sanction of law. California has recently passed its higher education law; Wisconsin and Washington are presently coming to grips with the issue and are both likely to pass a law in the near future. In those states where bargaining is not structured, the process often takes place in a jungle of muscle and clout, often accompanied by acrimonious struggles and job actions. This atmosphere is not conducive to positive, constructive, and stable employment relations nor to the adoption of good law.

Angell predicts that "by 1990, 60 to 70 percent of all faculty members are likely to be represented by unions." My prediction goes beyond this to something like 80-90 percent of the public-college faculties and perhaps 50-60 percent of the private higher education faculties (This in spite of the *Yeshiva* decision). As dollars get tighter and as college enrollments decrease, faculty will become more concerned about job security and they will increasingly concern themselves with collective action of one kind or another. If my predictions prove to be in the ballpark of accuracy, it would seem to indicate a strong need to accept this notion as a fact of collegiate life.

The Collective-Bargaining Process and Its Acceptance on Campus

In dealing with the current acceptance of the negotiating process by college administrators, Angell paints a rather dismal state of affairs.

Unfortunately, few college presidents conceal their abhorrence of the possibility that union organizers may come to campus. Most admit privately that they do everything possible to keep unions off campus including the improvement of salaries, perquisites, and personnel procedures.

Feelings among administrators who work with unionized faculties run the gamut from outright hatred of unions to a reasonable acceptance of unions as a fact of life. Those who accept the concept of faculty unionism, in my judgment, represent less than 10 percent and perhaps less than 5 percent of the total.

First I tend to agree with Angell's assessment, but I would like to inject some of my own thoughts as to the nature of collegial collective bargaining that must be understood before substantial progress on this front can be made.

In my ten years as chairman of the New York Public Employment Relations Board, I doubt that there is anyone who has advocated with more vigor than I the position that collective bargaining in higher education is, and indeed should be, a fundamentally different process than the traditional collective bargaining of the industrial model. While fully realizing the distinction between public and private colleges and universities, that distinction has tended to blur as more and more public monies come to private colleges. In fact, it has become difficult to tell with precision whether a college is public or private.

The normal distinction between the public and private sectors is drawn by separating the economic world of business and industry from the political world of government, paid for by taxes of various kinds. As previously indicated, when such a delineator is applied to higher education, the line becomes fuzzy, and I submit also that the operation within the various political constituencies of the private college and university becomes markedly similar to those of the public university. The legislative bodies may differ in nature and structure, but a board of trustees takes on many of the political attributes of a governmental legislative body.

There is no one single collective-bargaining system for higher education. In fact, there are almost as many systems as there are institutions. This is a major part of the uniqueness of higher education. The diversity of the various institutions, as well as the means by which these institutions are administered, create, of necessity, variations in the whole governance/collective-bargaining structure.

If there is any doctrine I would like to advocate, it is the doctrine of flexibility—flexibility in a carefully studied and reasoned response to the elements I have described. As faculty, administration, students, or sponsors of an institution face the issue of whether they will move into some system of collective bargaining, they must resist thinking in terms of black-and-white answers. Instead, a thorough study of the entire structure of the institution together with its administration should be made, and then changes should be made for the good of all concerned. It may very well be that the conclusions of such a study would be that the present governance structure is adequate for collective-bargaining purposes, or perhaps would be with certain modifications. It may be that the present governance structure will continue to oversee policy issues while some form of collective bargaining will be introduced to work with conditions of employment. There may be a host of other conclusions that would result from such a study. In a case between the *American Association of University Professors and Rutgers University* [2 NJPER 15 (1976)], the New Jersey Public Employment Relations Commission did not argue for the complete elimination of traditional governance by any means:

> As viewed by the Commission, . . . there is no reason why the systems of collegiality and collective negotiations may not function harmoniously. Neither system need impose upon the other, with one exception: terms and conditions of employment including grievances. The University is free to continue to delegate to collegial entities whatever managerial functions it chooses, subject, of course, to applicable law. The Act is among the laws applicable to a University as a public employer, and therefore collective negotiations under the Act would only mandate a change in the collegial system if that system were to operate so as to alter the University's obligation to deal exclusively with the AAUP with regard to the grievances and terms and conditions of employment of unit employees. Beyond that, both systems are free to operate without necessarily interfering with one another.

What we are really discussing is a system of communication between people and the organizations responsible for the management of the institution, the employees, and the students who are the recipients of its services. Unilateral management is a thing of the past. The whole idea that management will decide on a unilateral basis what is good for its employees—and if the employees do not like the decisions, they can move elsewhere—has long been obsolete. What is required is a viable system of shared decision making. This is the trademark of our modern society. Citizens of our society increasingly insist on a voice in the decisions that vitally affect their lives and the process by which these decisions are made.

Some professionals in the field contend that collective bargaining is a singular system of synchronizing the moods, demands, and needs of employers with those of the employees. They contend that any true collective-bargaining system must use the tools of pressure for agreement, threat of a strike, or actual strike or lockout; any system not using these tactics is not true collective bargaining. I reject that position. I believe that collective bargaining is not such a singular system. Rather, I believe there are, or should be, as many varieties of collective bargaining as there are businesses and industries and, closer to home, colleges and universities. There is nothing sacred about the term "collective bargaining." What it means is some type of appropriate employee involvement in the decision-making process regarding conditions of employment.

Most college administrators understandably have a strong aversion to any form of collective bargaining. In fact, many individual administrators as well as some administrative organizations refuse to sit down with representatives of faculty unions for fear that to do so will be considered a tacit acceptance of the concept. This was brought home forcibly when a group of about seventy-five prestigious leaders in higher education gathered at the 56th American Assembly of Columbia University at Arden House and discussed the subject, "The Integrity of Higher Education." Under the heading, "Public Perceptions," the Assembly stated:

> The public correctly or incorrectly believes that there is waste in its universities and colleges; they hear of tenure and conclude that it has become a job-security device for both the incompetent as well as the competent; they read inflated claims regarding faculty and curriculum only to find that one study program is like another; they suspect that collective bargaining will impair collegiality, drive up costs and lead to prolonged strikes.

Among the recommendations resulting from the discussions was the following:

> Because unionization is frequently destructive of the collegiality and academic standards essential to institutional integrity, faculty should, wherever possible, direct their efforts toward achieving effective participation in institutional governance by other means.

Thus it is fair to state that in spite of the rapid growth of some type of collective negotiations on the campuses of the nation, many administrators have not accepted the reality of the situation and hope that somehow it will go away. This does not appear to be a likely prospect; it is short-sighted and likely to be counterproductive.

The Success of Collective Bargaining and Its Effects on Higher Education

The alarmists and the prophets of gloom and doom who viewed with dismay the advent of collective bargaining in higher education have not seen their predictions materialize. As previously indicated, many leaders went so far as to claim that this development would not only interfere with the mission of the university, but some claimed it would lead to disintegration and destruction.

Angell deals rationally and objectively with two phases of this question—(1) Have faculty unions been successful? and (2) What overall effects have occurred to higher education as a result of faculty bargaining?

With regard to the success realization by faculty unions, Angell lists the six major objectives of faculty unions. I find no fault with this listing nor with Angell's conclusion:

If these six items represent a reasonably accurate statement of union objectives across the nation, I would have to conclude that most unions have been successful. Although studies comparing salaries at unionized and nonunionized campuses have been widely criticized for technical deficiencies, the weight of evidence indicates that unions, especially during the initial years of negotiation, have clearly improved salaries and fringe benefits.

The realization of this success, however, has not destroyed the traditional systems of governance. Both systems have been modified, adjusted, and adapted to each other. In a paper I presented before the annual meeting of the National Center for Collective Bargaining in Higher Education in New York City, I presented the following list of six major factors that tend to determine the nature and extent of these modifications to the bargaining process in higher education:

1. The nature of the college or university and the system of governance.
2. The history, development, and traditions of the higher education institution itself.
3. The academic structure and system within which the institution operates.
4. The locus of power in decision making.
5. The political needs of the various constituencies.
6. State, regional, and local differences.

With regard to the second phase in chapter 1—that of the effect of bargaining on higher education and its mission—again I cannot argue with Angell's major conclusions:

> My general assessment is that faculty bargaining has had little impact on the means of education that I generally classify under such rubrics as the quality of the faculty, of the student body, of the laboratories and libraries, and the availability of resources. Obviously, then, there appears to be as yet little effect on the ends of higher education such as the quality and performance of graduates, the research of faculty members, and other public services performed by the university.

I am not the authority in this facet since I left the ranks of higher education more than a dozen years ago, and much of whatever impact has occurred has been in these intervening years. However, other scholars who have studied this impact tend to agree with Angell. For example, Dr. James Begin of Rutgers University, who has studied collective bargaining in higher education has perhaps written as extensively as anyone on the subject has concluded,

> A major conclusion of this review, which will not be surprising to students of collective bargaining, is that the bargaining process in higher education is a reactive process shaping itself in relation to underlying environmental and organizational factors. Therefore, it is not surprising

to find that higher education bargaining has accommodated traditional governance and student concerns within its framework by shaping procedural and substantive outcomes unique to higher education.[1]

From my own observation from outside higher education, I would conclude that collective bargaining has been integrated with the varying governance systems in a wide variety of ways. The concern and authority of traditional governance mechanisms has tended to diminish in such areas of faculty economic and personnel policies. Curriculum issues, budget matters, physical facilities, student issues, and administrator selection are rarely found in faculty agreements and have largely been left to whatever governance system exists. Faculties are learning to have a meaningful voice in determining the conditions of employment, but this voice is being integrated into the university structure without unduly infringing on the mission of higher education or its traditional shared-management role.

Accommodating the Bargaining Process in the Future

While a certain amount of crystal-ball gazing is inherent in attempting to predict the future, such prophesy is assisted greatly by a close examination of what has happened in the past, together with the trends that have developed. Picking up on a number of the points made in chapter 1, I will deal quickly with (1) the process, (2) the role of the neutrals, particularly the administrative boards, commissions, and agencies that administer the collective-bargaining laws, (3) the role of the parties, (4) the relationship between the parties, (5) the role of the courts, and (6) the challenge to the leadership of higher education. Because of the length of the list, comments will necessarily be brief.

The Process

We have dealt at length with the societal changes that have brought some form of collective negotiations into being. Employees in every walk of life want to be involved in making the critical decisions that affect their lives. This is particularly true with education where professionals feel that they possess an expertise that should be utilized and pooled for the overall good of the organization. I see no let-up in this trend. Governance and bargaining will continue to interrelate and be adapted to each other in as wide a variety of mechanisms as there are colleges and universities. The process may often bear little resemblance to the traditional bargaining model of business and industry.

Angell's position seems to concur with this outlook as he observes,

Tradition now seems to favor extension of labor rights to public employees everywhere ... My contacts with administrators, trustees, union representatives, and legislators in several regions of the country predict thát attention to labor legislation in every state of the union, with the exception perhaps of North Carolina, is increasing every year. . . . Several states that now have meet-and-confer laws are feeling strong pressure for bona-fide labor legislation requiring written agreements between the parties.

Additionally, the significant differences between unions and professional organizations are gradually disappearing; and as a result, the distinctions among such terms as "collective negotiations," "collective bargaining," and "meet and confer," are also fading. As the process is better understood, the technicalities of nomenclature and the intricacies of procedural matters become less important. What really matters is what happens within the organization to achieve a reasonable balance among the legitimate needs and interests of the employees, the students, the employer and the several constituencies who are responsible for the funds, policies and success of the enterprise.

The Role of Neutrals

Chapter 1 is relatively critical of the governmental administrative agencies that have been called on to administer the laws in the various states. It is also critical of legislative bodies and government executives where the "traditional separation of public higher education from state politics has been all but destroyed, and it will be up to future historians to assess the effects."

I accede to a certain amount of the naïveté and ignorance suggested by Angell and have a certain sympathy for the higher education enterprise that witnessed one more arm of government intruding into what had heretofore been left to the control of the enterprise itself. Boards such as New York's Public Employment Relations Board were given sweeping laws that extended collective-bargaining rights to all public employees for the first time. There was little precedent other than the experience of the National Labor Relations Act, the decisions of the National Labor Relations Board, and the courts—much of which were considered inappropriate in the new world of public-employment labor relations.

In spite of this challenge, however, I would give these agencies better grades than Angell has. I submit that many of the problems emanated from higher education itself. Administrators and boards of trustees did not understand the process and tended to equate it with strikes; they confined their efforts largely to how they could keep unionism out and defeat faculty attempts to organize. The collegial world had previously few professionals who understood labor relations in higher education and who were prepared to represent administration in any enlightened manner. Higher education did not know what to do with their faculty senates and other governance mechanisms in the light of the new developments; many even tried to transform these mechanisms into employee organizations. On the employee side, faculty and their organizations were equally confused. They were very uncertain about the effect of bargaining on governance; they did not know whether they should try to retain their governance structure for policy issues while utilizing the bargaining system for determination of conditions of employment; their professional organizations were very unsure whether they wanted to become employee organizations in the traditional sense, or whether they should stay with governance and leave collective bargaining to the unions. These are just a few of the uncertainties that literally took years to resolve. In New York it took the state university three or four years to begin to get definite answers to these and many related questions; many of the answers to these questions are still not clear. It was hard enough for new governmental agencies to be suddenly thrust into this new world of public-employment labor relations; but difficulties were compounded immeasurably by these unique uncertainties in higher education. Given the legislative mandates and the lack of preparation that existed, the agencies have done surprisingly well. This in no way indicates that they do not have a lot to learn and a long way to go. That in fact is the thrust of my present project, the Public Employment Relations Services, a project that is committed to raising the level of professional competence of these agencies.

If there is any recommendation I would stress above any other, it is to plead with higher education to learn what collective negotiations is all about instead of simply defying and resisting unions and unionism. I am not suggesting that higher education necessarily encourage or acquiesce to the system of bargaining. I do suggest that whatever directions are pursued should emerge out of enlightenment and understanding rather than out of blind adherence to tradition and emotional reaction.

The Role of the Parties in Bargaining

Experience has demonstrated that when parties first engage in some kind of collective negotiations, there is often a drawing of lines and a choosing of "sides" by management and employees. This practice is unproductive and tends to be compounded by the employers resistance to what they feel is inappropriate intrusion into their rights to manage the university. Many times a spirit of intense acrimony develops in adversarial proceedings.

Angell tends to be optimistic in looking for a decreased amount of this kind of emotionalism:

> I predict that as administrators learn how to work with union leaders during the eighties, they will find union channels at least as timely and responsive as the usual faculty senate and more decisive. By 1990 unions will find it less rewarding to attack administrators, and most grievances will be processed routinely and with little publicity. Petty grievances will receive summary attention because they will have become more of a nuisance to unions than to administrators.

I could not say it better. However, for this kind of enlightenment to take place, there are two fundamental requirements, which are education and understanding on the part of all those involved—administrators, boards of trustees, legislative bodies, faculty, faculty representatives, and the neutrals who administer, mediate, fact-find, arbitrate, and decide cases. The courts must also undergo an increased understanding of both higher education and labor relations in the new setting. To be more specific, management, which is responsible for managing the funds to achieve the educational objectives, often has little or no understanding of the negotiations process that determines how perhaps 80-85 percent of total budgets will be used. There are no requirements in any of the states for educators, administrators, and leaders of the higher education enterprise to take even a most basic course in labor relations. In many states that require certification and/or licensing for education administrators, I know of none that requires any kind of basic training or experience in this field that is so vital to them. If administrators participate in any effort in connection with the negotiations process, that participation is likely limited to means by which they can resist or forestall unionism and prevent it from coming to their campuses. I believe that this is a head-in-the-sand approach, one that is shortsighted and counterproductive and indeed flies in the face of one of the basic tenets of higher education—that of learning to adapt appropriately to the dynamics of a world of certain change.

The parties themselves are often represented at the negotiations table by those who do not really understand the process, who do not understand higher education, or both. Universities need to accept the notion that a fundamental requirement will be to identify, train, and develop persons to manage their employment relations. Far too frequently the higher education establishment employs a so-called hired gun to negotiate a contract within the administrative policies. When this is completed, they feel they have discharged their responsibilities when, in fact, the most important part of that responsibility, namely, the administration of that contract, still remains. This world of change that academicians are so inclined to describe, make speeches and write papers about, has come to their own doorstep, and they must educate, train, and develop the staff to deal with this change with understanding and enlightenment. Carefully developed persuasion and reason must substitute for a battle of muscle, clout, and emotionalism.

The Relationship between the Parties

Administrative agencies—thirty-two of them now in the various states—have engaged in wide experimentation with various dispute-settlement techniques and procedures. This has been the single most innovative and exciting area of public-sector labor relations. While the private sector has relied on the right to strike as the ultimate weapon when parties failed to reach agreement, the legislature, the public, and the parties in the public sector have developed many forms of mediation, fact-finding, public hearings, arbitration, and combinations thereof. One of the most interesting developments of the last dozen years has been the combining of many of these procedures and techniques in every conceivable effort to extend the bargaining process and assist the parties in reaching agreement. In dealing with this subject, Angell speculates,

> A trend toward the use of interest arbitration, rather than strikes for settling negotiation deadlocks may reduce antiunion publicity. Unions traditionally have opposed arbitration because it ostensibly deprives them of their ultimate weapon, the strike. Strikes following arbitration almost always fail. Also employers generally abhor the right of a third party (arbiter) to determine how much of the budget must be spent on salaries and benefits. Growing public antipathy toward strikes, however, has led twenty-three states to make interest arbitration legal. Fire fighters and police unions now seek national law requiring arbitration. I believe that arbitration will almost completely replace the use of faculty strikes by the year 1990. Even liberal professors are, by and large, unwilling to strike for their own conditions of employment. Assured use of arbitration, a procedure more consistent with the principles of logic and reason that they teach, will make bargaining much more attractive to senior faculty members who have already achieved a measure of security.

Very few people in any phase of public employment have been willing to go this far. Public employers tend to resist interest arbitration strongly because they feel it represents an improper delegation of authority, a violation of the one-man-one-vote principle, a violation of home rule, and a lack of accountability of the arbitrator to the legislative body. Employee organizations are more and more favoring some form of arbitration over the right to strike since they feel that as governments and the public have adjusted to the strike, they have learned to substitute services and to manage and win strikes; thus the power of strikes has diminished in bringing about fair treatment and equity.

I agree with Angell in this assessment. It is encouraging that gradually we are learning better ways to reconcile differing points of view and bring about agreements. There are even now twenty-five or thirty different types of interest arbitration being used in twenty-two states. As legislative bodies face a choice between the trauma of strikes or the arbitration of these disputes as a last resort, slowly—and many times reluctantly—they move toward arbitration. When the teachers of Hortonville, Wisconsin, went on strike, the school board discharged them, hired new ones, and proceeded with school. After working through the courts, the Supreme Court of the United States decided that the school board had acted legally. The Wisconsin State Legislature has now adopted what amounts to a "med-arb" law that requires arbitration as the last step in dispute settlement for all public employees including teachers. As Wisconsin adds higher education to collective-bargaining coverage, it will be interesting to see whether they permit the extension of arbitration to higher education.

After 284 striking teachers in Bridgeport, Connecticut, were put in jail because they violated a court injunction that ordered them to cease their strike, the Connecticut Legislature adopted an arbitration law for its teachers.

Some six years ago at a White House Conference on the 1990s, I ventured the prediction that within perhaps twenty-five years, the strike would become as obsolete as the duel. If Angell and I are right in this projection, marked changes in attitude of the public are likely to occur toward collective bargaining. For example, approximately eight years ago, I recommended to the New York State Legislature a system of three-choice arbitration for teachers. Interestingly, people in Iowa read my testimony and subsequently adopted this system for all the state's public employees.

The Role of the Courts

As public-sector unionism has progressed, the courts have moved more aggressively into various facets of the process. They are going beyond the rights of private enterprise, beyond even the sacred rights of employees for due process and just cause. Increasingly, courts feel obliged to protect the democratic process of government. Particularly in the present and foreseeable economic climate, they have tended to become more conservative, restrictive, and protective of the rights of government. This assertion moves beyond Angell's contention. Angell projects that the courts will have a lot to do with the bargaining process (for example, *Yeshiva*). I not only agree but move one more step to believing that the courts will go much further and much more carefully into the public sector than they have in the private sector. Courts have become particularly conservative when dealing with scope of bargaining, government rights to manage, and anything having to do with interest arbitration.

The *Yeshiva* case has now been decided by the Supreme Court of the United States. The extreme management view will probably contend that *Yeshiva* will all but end collective bargaining in higher education. The extreme union view will probably indicate that the decision was carefully limited to the unique governance conditions of *Yeshiva*—a private university operating under the National Labor Relations Law. In my judgment, the *Yeshiva* decision will mean a great deal more litigation before clear directions are established. But it does exemplify the willingness of the courts to move into the higher education collective-bargaining equation with a note of real caution in doing so.

Another stellar example of this occurred recently in Minnesota where an arbitrator granted a raise of 18 percent to the faculty of a community college in a two-year contract. The state legislature reduced this to 14 percent. The faculty association took this to a lower court, and that court reversed the action of the legislature contending that since this resulted from an arbitration award, the legislature could not change it. The Supreme Court of Minnesota reversed the lower court, contending that the arbitrator's award becomes a part of the contract, and therefore the legislature was within its rights in changing that condition of employment. This represents a marked change in court directions when they hold that a legislative body can in effect change the substance of an arbitrator's award.

The Challenge to the Leadership of Higher Education

The last five pages of chapter 1 pull together Angell's assessment of where we are likely headed in the next decade of experience with collective bargaining in higher education. It is the voice of the eternal optimist, particularly in his assessment of 1995 and beyond:

> In conclusion, it is my conviction that mature faculty unions of the nineties will look and act like long-established faculty senates and that, to their own surprise, many college presidents will accept union presence as a normal collegial-type operation.

> Once achieved, educators will no longer be interested in questioning the validity of unions in the profession of education; rather, they will be debating the proper use of educational-political power in shaping public policy beyond academic borders.

The thrust of these final pages seems to go like this: If the negotiation process has become a fact of life for higher education, and I think it has, why not learn to use it appropriately to the mutual benefit of the employees, the students, the institution, and the public it is designed to serve? The call is for enlightened leadership in higher education that will lead the way toward this objective. After all, the faculty is fully as interested and committed to the success of the mission of the university as is the administration. Understanding can largely dispel the acrimony and emotionalism of adversarial relationships. The adaptation of the process to the unique nature of higher education can succeed in harnessing the total resources of the university, administration, faculty, and students toward a more effective achievement of its mission. I subscribe enthusiastically to this doctrine.

Note

1. James P. Begin, "Higher Education," *Portrait of a Process—Collective Negotiations in Public Employment* (Fort Washington, Penn.: Labor Relations Press, 1979), pp. 389-407.

5 Commentary

David Kuechle

In late 1974 Dr. Malcolm Seitz was named as the fourteenth president of Midstate University after the trustees' year-long search. He would assume his new position on 1 July 1975. The trustees of Midstate, once one of the country's most prestigious universities, selected Dr. Seitz largely because they believed his wide renown as a scientist and his connections in important circles of government, at home and overseas, would help attract higher-quality students and faculty and would bring new money to the institution: money to be used for research, increased faculty salaries, and an ambitious building program.

Initial reactions to Dr. Seitz's appointment were gratifying. Students, faculty, and alumni were nearly unanimous in their enthusiasm, and new money started to flow almost immediately as friends and alumni rallied proudly to support their alma mater.

Within a few months after Dr. Seitz assumed the presidency, it became clear that he was interested in using the position to enhance his personal ambitions. He traveled frequently, often abroad, and he readily accepted consulting assignments and nonpaying appointments to high-level study commissions in government and foundations. He entertained lavishly at university expense, and he issued frequent statements for publication about U.S. foreign policy, the economic situation, scientific developments and, on occasion, about higher education: its problems and its future. All of these ventures brought considerable notoriety to the university and Dr. Seitz. However, Seitz was away from the campus most of the time, and he paid little attention to his own university—leaving day-to-day matters for handling by subordinates, many of whom were continued from the earlier president's regime. The situation was especially difficult because Seitz himself brought along an entourage of associates whose responsibilities seemed to duplicate many of the holdovers. Administrative overlap and confusion were rampant.

Seitz did not monitor the quality or relevance of the school's educational programs and did nothing to nurture or enhance endowments, to attract more funds for research, to plan for new facilities, or to build administrative competence in the organization. Within three years it was evident that the university was in trouble. Enrollments declined, and so did the quality of entering students. Research money that once came to Midstate seemed to be going elsewhere, and the institution was rapidly moving toward financial chaos. Some highly respected faculty members started to look elsewhere for positions, and when several of them resigned, the trustees stepped in and announced that drastic steps would be taken. As a first step, all salaries would be frozen. Beyond that, no faculty member would be granted a sabbatical leave until further notice. Then the chairman of the board announced that several experimental teaching programs would be cut, and at least one graduate school would be shut down. As a result of these measures, total faculty size would be reduced, and remaining faculty members would be asked to take on greater workloads—with no added compensation.

Dr. Seitz was asked to resign, but not before the faculty had unionized. And the reasons for unionization were not much different than reasons for unionization among employees in offices and factories. The faculty members feared for their own security, and they wanted to protect their rapidly dwindling earning power. Some of them said they wanted a greater role in managing the university—to take over the functions that they believed Dr. Seitz and the rest of the administration had so badly fumbled.

This account is disguised, but it is based on a real situation, and it illustrates an important fact—that college and university administrators who are perceived by faculty members to be squandering money, not planning wisely, and threatening the future of the institution, can reasonably expect to foment faculty unrest. In some instances there will be pressure to unionize because faculty members who have devoted substantial parts of their working life to the institution are not likely to let someone else destroy the place!

There has been an enormous growth of unions among college and university faculties in the last decade, and this can be attributed in large part to administrators like Dr. Seitz who have managed badly—so badly that members of the faculty came to believe that they had to assume a more active role in management, and, where necessary, to assert their collective power in the interest of collective security. Unionism became the vehicle for doing this.

So it was at Yeshiva University in New York where faculty members voted overwhelmingly in 1976 to be certified as a union. Their grievances were numerous: Among them were two unilaterally imposed salary freezes—both announced without prior consultation with faculty members. In 1975-1976, faculty members were particularly incensed when they learned that the vice president of business affairs received a salary *increase* exceeding 9 percent during the freeze, giving him an annual income of over $50,000, more than twice the average salary of full professors in the union. In addition, Yeshiva increased faculty teaching loads from twelve to fifteen hours a week, changed sabbatic leave policies, and changed criteria for retirement benefits. In 1977 Yeshiva closed a graduate school, the Belfer School of Science, with no prior warning to students and faculty who were involved. Faculty members, frustrated in the belief that they had no meaningful input into any of these decisions, unionized, and their fight lasted for more than seven years.

Two hundred miles northeast of New York, the faculty at another university, Boston University, formed a union for many of the same reasons that prevailed at Yeshiva. Most of all, they wanted to protect themselves against their administration, symbolized by President John Silber. Silber, a tough man, had set out to improve the quality of the institution and build its financial strength. In the process, all the university's vice presidents were replaced, as were all but one dean and thirty-eight of the fifty-three department chairpersons. In addition, an early-retirement program was implemented so that department chairpersons could more easily get rid of "dead wood" on the faculty. While these actions may have been designed to enhance the best interests of the university, they sowed seeds of distrust among a substantial number of faculty members who perceived the actions to be arbitrary and capricious—even ruthless. So they formed a union. After five years of organizing activity, including NLRB hearings and court battles, Boston University faculty members finally achieved a contract with the administration in May of 1979.

If we examine the 384 unionized faculties in the country, we will find many examples similar to those at Midstate, Yeshiva, and Boston University. Nevertheless, there are reasons to believe that the growth rate of faculty unions has peaked, and, as in private industry during the last two decades, there will be a decline in the number of faculty unions over the next ten years. In the short run, as a result of the *Yeshiva* decision, there may be a sharp decline. The *Yeshiva* case, decided by the Supreme Court on 20 February 1980, held that Yeshiva University was not obligated to bargain with its faculty union because the faculty, according to the Court, are managerial employees. As such, they are exempt from coverage of the National Labor Relations Act.[1]

Since jurisdiction of the National Labor Relations Act extends only to private colleges and universities, the decision had no immediate impact on the 120,000 or so unionized faculty members in the public sector, most of whom are covered by state labor laws. However, most state laws are patterned after the national act, and many of them exclude managerial employees from coverage. So it is reasonable to assume that some administrators in colleges and universities in the public and private sectors alike will refuse to bargain with their faculties for the same reason that Yeshiva refused—claiming that they have managerial authority and, as such, are not entitled to be represented by unions.[2] Turmoil resulting from such actions will last for several years as courts throughout the country determine the extent of *Yeshiva's* impact.

While action is taking place in the courts, we can also expect action on the legislative front. There will be moves by unions to change the labor-relations laws so that they *specifically* provide for faculty bargaining. These of course will be fought by some college and university administrators and possibly by employer-oriented lobbying groups such as the National Right-to-Work committee. Some of these fights will be long and bitter.

Within the cloistered world of higher education, it is generally acknowledged that Yeshiva's faculty had very little managerial power when compared to other faculties in higher education. For this reason, *Yeshiva* appeared to be a poor test case for colleges and universities. There is no faculty senate at Yeshiva—never had been—and the administration maintains veto power over recommendations by the faculty regarding the status of colleagues. Nevertheless, the court ruled that Yeshiva's faculty members play a crucial role in operating the enterprise. In the many institutions where the faculty's managerial role is greater than at Yeshiva, faculty unions may now be living on borrowed time.

The *Yeshiva* ruling will not serve to erase grievances that gave rise to union activity there or elsewhere. And as long as administrators like those at Midstate University, Boston University, and Yeshiva are perceived by faculty members to be acting contrary to the best interests of the institution, there will be pressure to unionize—with or without protection of the law. Some faculty unions will derive new-found strength from the fact that they are *not* protected by the law. They will look to the experience of other unions that have grown and prospered outside the protection of labor laws. Two examples of such unions are the (1) International Association of Masters, Mates, and Pilots and (2) the Marine Engineers Beneficial Association. The majority of members in these unions are acknowledged to be managers, and there is no protection for them under the labor laws. However, both of these unions have great strength and are formidable bargaining organizations. They forced voluntary recognition by employers in many cases even before passage of the National Labor Relations Act. Subsequent to passage of the act, they maintained their strength, sometimes by resorting to tactics that would probably be unfair labor practices under the labor laws. But employers were hindered in fighting such tactics because the law denied protection to them as well as to the unions. Where grievances were sufficient to cause masters, mates, pilots, and marine engineers to organize, they did it—notwithstanding the absence of protective laws. It grievances are severe enough to cause faculty members like those at Yeshiva to fight for seven years to gain recognition, it is reasonable to believe that if protection under the law is denied, faculty members will resort to tactics similar to those that helped build formidable extralegal bargaining organizations.

The Supreme Court's *Yeshiva* decision did not close the door to faculty unions even under the present National Labor Relations Act. The majority opinion suggested that a line might be drawn between tenured and untenured faculty—that the latter might not perform managerial functions in some institutions and could be eligible for protection under the labor act. Unions can be expected to pursue this suggestion and attempt to carve out bargaining units of nontenured faculty for representation. In doing so, they could have an even more divisive effect on universities and colleges. It is quite possible, for example, that nontenured faculty members will organize to bargain with their tenured colleagues (as managers) over such issues as promotion, merit raises, academic freedom, and even tenure itself.

It is expected then that there will be a decline in faculty-union activity in the wake of the *Yeshiva* decision. Then there will be regrouping, and a vigorous resurgence of organizing activity will take place. Its character will change: There will be more attention paid to legislation, more attention to seeking recognition by extralegal means, and more attention to carving out faculty units that split those who have managerial responsibility (perhaps the tenured ranks) from those that do not. All this points to uncertainty and turmoil for the next several years.

Yeshiva notwithstanding, there is reason to believe that faculty unions will decline in number during the second half of the 1980s and eventually level off at a percentage that reflects the general percentage of union members throughout the country. There are three important reasons for making this prediction:

The declining nature of the industry

Smarter managements

The distinctive characteristics of faculty members

Declining Nature of the Industry

Enrollment declines, retrenchment, and fewer jobs have led to faculty-unionization drives in the name of job security. So too has failure to maintain earning levels that compare favorably to unionized workers in other walks of life. But drives that are calculated to alleviate these conditions will be short-lived.

In the period of 1967 to 1978, college professors experienced a drop in real salaries of 9.6 percent. During the same period unionized steelworkers increased their earning power, even in the face of inflation, by nearly 35 percent. Coal miners upped theirs by 31 percent.[3] Although average salaries of steelworkers and coal miners on one hand and professors on the other are still fairly wide apart (in favor of professors), professors are aware of the closing gap, which has exerted pressure on them to unionize. However, it has become apparent that faculty unions looking for whopping increases in pay do not carry much weight in the face of fiscal restraints brought about by Proposition 13 fever. Cries among public-sector employees in state legislatures about austerity programs, decreasing numbers of jobs, and declining earning power are all having less and less impact, especially in the field of higher education. The enthusiasm that stimulated union activity in the 1970s has rapidly been cooled.

Prosperity years for colleges and universities are over, and politicians who want to stay in office must make decisions on how to allocate limited resources based on some important developments in this regard. One development, for example, concerns the number of citizens in the group usually considered to be college eligible. The eighteen to twenty-one age group had 17.1 million members in 1979. From now on, barring massive immigration, this age group will decline, hitting 15.4 million in 1985, 14.5 million in 1990, and 13.0 million in 1995. Fifteen years from now the number of Americans of college age will be 75 percent of what it is today, assuming that there are no major shifts in the average age of people attending colleges.

The percentage of high school graduates, which until now has provided the basic pool of college aspirants, will probably not increase. Significant upward changes in high school completion rates took place in the 1960s when the drive for equal opportunity for minorities was going full speed. In the years 1970–1975 the rate of high school completions was almost constant—about 75 percent. However, the current concern over academic standards in our school systems and the likelihood of more competency testing might have a depressing effect on the number of high school students who graduate, and there is no reason to believe that the percentage of graduates going on to college (now about 60 percent) will change. Some colleges and universities have attempted to counterbalance the decline in the eighteen to twenty-one year age group by adopting new programs in adult education, life-long learning, and part-time programs. However, there is little likelihood that these will have a significant countervailing effect.

From winter 1970 through summer 1978, over 250 colleges and universities have closed. Among independent institutions alone 129 closed, 42 merged, and 17 shifted to public control. While these 188 independent institutions were losing their identities, 64 new ones were founded, for a net loss of 124.[4] All that, coupled with a declining popular image of higher education, suggests that there is not much likelihood that favorable attention will be given by politicians to college faculties—unionized or not—who ask for more! For this reason, many current union-organizing drives among faculty will be short-lived.

Throughout history there has been a close correlation between the rate of unionization and stages of the economic cycle. When economic conditions were bad and unemployment high, the union movement suffered. On the other hand, when the employment picture brightened and employers were able to pay more, unions flourished. The reason: They were able to produce benefits for their members, to show results. A union that cannot deliver on its promises soon dies.

Since passage of the National Labor Relations Act in 1935 and subsequent passage of various pieces of social-welfare legislation, workers have received greater protection from economic downturns than they had before. Thus the peaks and valleys are not as great for workers as they used to be. However, colleges and universities reached an all-time peak in prosperity and employment in the early 1970s. A serious downturn is now upon us. The number of unemployed Ph.D.s is at an all-time high. Those colleges and universities that were fiscally marginal may face extinction if they respond to normal union pressures for more money and greater job security—carrying faculty unions and their members along. Those that hold the line and possibly face strike action will likely jeopardize their market, as students go elsewhere. And those that survive are not likely to do it by giving in to large union demands. Thus in the short run faculty unions will find rough sledding. If they do score short-run gains, the long-term impact could be devastating. Regardless of the political power unions may have, that which is in possession of various *faculty* unions is meager in legislative halls where decisions are being made regarding who among employees will get the greatest slice of the pie. Until now, NEA, AAUP, and AFT have had difficulty in resolving their own internecine battles, thereby sapping strength that might otherwise help develop a common front to compete effectively with The American Federation of State, County, and Municipal Employees, SEIU, the Teamsters, and other major public-sector unions for declining resources.

Smarter Managements

The second important reason why faculty unionism in colleges and universities will decline lies in the fact that managements are getting smarter. They are better able to defeat union drives, if they want to, and they are more knowledgeable about how to create conditions so that faculty members will not feel a need to unionize.

The administration at Yeshiva University demonstrated in textbook fashion how a union-organization drive can be frustrated and eventually defeated. Back in 1973 Yeshiva's president refused voluntary recognition to the university's faculty union. Then later the university challenged the composition of the proposed faculty bargaining unit—arguing for over five months for the exclusion of each dean, each department chairperson, each researcher, each principal investigator, each part-time employee. Their case was handled by a full-time labor attorney (not the general counsel), assisted by various outside labor lawyers. Later the university succeeded in getting two postponements of the representation election. As an added element, there was an unfair-labor-practice charge by a faculty member, apparently choreographed by someone in the administration. The charge itself was against the university, but in a bizarre twist of the law, it helped the university by delaying the organization drive. Throughout the campaign the university engaged in vigorous letter-writing campaigns. Numerous letters were signed by President Norman Lamm and sent to the homes of faculty members urging them to throw aside the union.

After the union won the NLRB election in December of 1976, the university refused to bargain, creating conditions for an unfair-labor-practice charge by the faculty. Hearings were held before the National Labor Relations Board and in subsequent court appeals, each handled by labor experts who had a wealth of experience.

Yeshiva's actions were dictated by a clear administrative policy laid out by the president, backed by the board of trustees, and adhered to by the entire administrative staff. The policy was dictated by the belief that unionization of faculty members at Yeshiva would lead to an adversary, legalistic relationship that would be unsuited to the academic community. It followed logically for Yeshiva that every possible effort should be exerted to prevent unionization. Other college and university administrations who wish to fight their faculties now can be guided by the Yeshiva model.

The president and trustees at Boston University (BU) shared the same belief about faculty unions as those that guided Yeshiva, and while the BU faculty finally achieved recognition and negotiated a first contract in the spring of 1979, their situation is now tenuous. BU can be expected to terminate their bargaining relationship as soon as the current collective-bargaining agreement expires.

During the 1970s, top administrators in colleges and universities were collectively ignorant about unions. Most college presidents were not trained in matters of management. Coming from backgrounds in the sciences, engineering, anthropology, philosophy, and the arts, they were viewed as intellectual leaders—not managers of substantial business establishments. Those colleges and universities that employed counsel with general legal background relied on that counsel when union-organizing drives came about and, by and large, they received poor advice. For example, they were regularly advised to say nothing and do nothing during an organizing drive, lest they get hit with an unfair-labor-practice charge. An experienced labor counsel would not give that advice to administrators who wish to fight unionization. He or she would know that managements can say and do many things during an organizing drive that would not be termed unfair labor practices. He or she would also know that most penalties for unfair labor practices are not severe.

Now after more than a decade of faculty unionization and with increased awareness of rights and responsibilities in relationships with unions, managements in our nation's colleges and universities have become wise through experience. In addition, more and more top administrators in colleges and universities are going back to school to train themselves to be effective managers. It is no accident that in the past four years labor relations is the subject receiving greatest allocation of class time in Harvard's Institute for Educational Management and Stanford's Management Institute for College and University Officers. The principal focus of these labor-relations courses has been on faculty unions. Presidents, vice presidents, chancellors, and deans are learning how to deal with faculty unions—to defeat or weaken them if they so desire or to work with them toward accommodation if that is what they want. They have learned that professional advisers are available to help do either and, most importantly, they have learned to develop and implement policies in the field of labor relations that are tied closely to the general policies of the organization. Labor relations is no longer something for unattached experts to worry about. College presidents and trustees now know that labor-relations decisions are critical for the organization. In fact, they may spell the difference between survival and demise.

Most college and university administrators empathize with their faculties. Many were faculty members themselves, and the often understand the concerns that gave rise to faculty unionism. For the most part, they want to work with their faculties to alleviate those concerns—to create conditions so that faculty members will not want to organize. We often hear college presidents and trustees express the desire for greater collegiality, wherein faculty members and administrators work closely together toward common objectives, where peer reviews determine questions of promotion and tenure, and where important decisions about adding new programs, dropping subject areas, and expanding or contracting physical facilities are shared. In such arrangements there is no clear distinction between managers and those who are managed. There may be arguments, but most of these focus on shared objectives.

Many college and university administrators do not believe that a collegial style of management can coexist with a unionized faculty. They believe that unions are adversarial bodies and must stay that way in order to survive. This belief is borne out when, in negotiations, unions usually want more than the institution is willing to give. Often represented by outsiders, unionized faculty do not seem to share objectives in the same vein as the administration.

Other administrators believe that a unionized faculty offers a structured opportunity to build a collegial relationship—that unions force administrators to account for their decisions—to keep accurate, up-to-date records, to operate in such a way that there will be no charges of capriciousness, incompetence, or discrimination. Through grievance procedures, unions and managements can often hammer out solutions that are in everyone's best interest. Sometimes, in a mature relationship, the union assumes the role of a faculty senate, and collegiality emerges.

Wherever a college or university administrator stands on the spectrum of views about faculty unionization, he or she now has the knowledge and skills to create a relationship that will have a chilling effect on unionization. If an administrator stands on the *Yeshiva* end of the spectrum, he or she knows about and is willing to use all tools to frustrate unionization. If he or she is on the other end of the spectrum and sees the union as an opportunity to develop a collegial method of operating, there will be less and less reason for the union itself to exist. Formal grievances will largely disappear, and decisions that might result in sacrifice of job security or earning power will be matters for codetermination. There will not be an adversary to blame! Under such conditions it will be difficult to get faculty members to pay much attention to their union any more, let alone pay dues. Rather, they will mostly return to the things they like to do best: to teach, do research, write, and be left alone.

Associate Professor Paul Connolly of Yeshiva College, one of the principal organizers of the faculty union there, blamed the faculty itself for letting administrators take too much power, thereby creating a situation in which the faculty felt a need to abandon their other activities, at lease for awhile, to reestablish the institution as a supportive body.

> Now, when a faculty seeks to reclaim its authority, it faces the profound irony evident in the Yeshiva situation. We, the Yeshiva faculty, had to insist that we are non-managerial and non-supervisory in order to organize ourselves into a body that can reassert its managerial, supervisory authority. . . .[5]

The Triple-Edged Sword

The union movement among college and university faculties faces a triple-edged sword. On one edge they face administrators who are better able to defeat them because of greater knowledge and sophistication in dealing with the technicalities of organizing drives. On another edge they face administrators who are better able to create conditions in the absence of faculty unions that will make it unlikely that faculties will want to organize. And on the third edge of the sword are administrators who, in working with faculty unions, will develop collegial relations, thus eliminating the need for the union itself.

Distinctive Characteristics of Faculty Members

The third reason why faculty unionism will decline in colleges and universities involves the unique psyche of faculty members themselves. By and large, faculty members are members of a rare breed: one that enjoys great job satisfaction. Unlike clerical and factory workers who often find their work dull, repetitive, and confining, faculty members are largely free to do their own thing: to do research in areas of interest; to read, write, and teach their favorite subjects, to work in pleasant surroundings among stimulating people, and to be largely in control of their day-to-day activities.

Persons with these characteristics do not represent the stereotype of union activists. For the most part, they dislike table pounding, exchanging of demands, long meetings, and parading in picket lines. In recent years, however, many faculty members have done all these things—often surprising themselves in the process. Many of them, even the most militant, would rather get back to their own special interests, secure in the knowledge that the organization is sufficiently sound that they will not be hassled or threatened by incompetent administrators.

Faculty-union leaders are also getting smarter, along with administrators, and many have expressed a desire to establish a relationship wherein the union will act like a senate and where administrations will view the union as an instrument for excellence, where college administrators like those at Midstate

University (our disguised institution), Yeshiva University, and Boston University can sit side by side with their faculty representatives and engage in mutual problem solving while focusing on shared objectives.

Notes

1. *National Labor Relations Board* v. *Yeshiva University*, U.S. Supreme Court, Case No. 78-857, 103 LRRM 2526, February 20, 1980.

2. On March 8, 1980, the University of New Haven in Connecticut announced that it was terminating contract negotiations with its faculty union, citing the *Yeshiva* case as its reason. The faculty union at New Haven had been in existence for four years and was negotiating its third contract.

3. Paul Blumberg, "White-collar Status Panic," *The New Republic*, December 1, 1979, pp. 21-23.

4. Office of Research, National Institute of Independent Colleges and Universities, Research Report, December 1978.

5. Paul H. Connolly, "Faculty Members: Hired Hands or Managers?" *The Chronicle of Higher Education*, September 25, 1978, p. 40.

6

Does Teacher Bargaining Affect Student Achievement?

Robert E. Doherty

Most people who have bothered to look into the matter at all have concluded that public education in America faces serious difficulties. Student achievement is down, costs are up, and public dissatisfaction with education appears to be at an all-time high. These difficulties began in the mid 1960s, about the same time teachers started to organize for collective-bargaining purposes, and it is the contention of many that bargaining has contributed to the problem. It is possible that those who see this connection just might have a point, although I believe the influence of bargaining on educational costs and performance to be modest, and even then probably impossible to document.

There is also a certain amount of confusion as to what the outcome of public education ought to be. Clearly we are concerned that the schools do more than develop cognitive skills. The rub is that there is little agreement as to what other things ought to be done. Moreover, just about every parent agrees that instruction in reading, writing, and ciphering are important tasks for teachers to perform, and how well students achieve in these areas is probably the best measure available on how good a job the schools are doing. One hears many school administrators claim that training in the cognitive skills is, or ought to be, less important than it once was, that instead the schools ought to emphasize such matters as improving international understanding, increasing the appreciation of other cultures and other life styles. A school superintendent recently told me that his proudest achievement as a school administrator was that he was able to persuade his school board to remove "training in the basic skills" from the foremost goal of the school system and have moved up into its place something called, "training in life-long learning." How students were expected to become life-long learners if they lacked the skills for learning in the first place is evidently a matter deemed unworthy of consideration. A cynic would argue that the emphasis given such subtopics as "values clarification" and "life adjustment" are not merely the products of addled school officials but rather an attempt to obfuscate the real issue: Students are achieving less well than in previous years. It follows that if school officials are incapable of reversing that trend, they must then argue that achievement in the cognitive domain is not that important after all. Critics of public education are thereby silenced since there is no way to measure the effectiveness of the schools when they undertake to teach what cannot be measured.

The evidence on the achievement of U.S. public school students *is* distressing. Average Scholastic Aptitude Test (SAT) math scores declined from 485 in the mid 1960s to 465 in 1978. There was an even sharper decline in average verbal ability during the same period, as measured by the SATs: from 470 to 425. It is important to note here that this decline cannot be attributed to more difficult tests or a change in the socioeconomic mix of the test takers. Harnischfeger and Wiley have pointed out that the socioeconomic mix of test takers has remained constant over the past several years and that the SATs have actually become easier. Indeed, these analysts estimate that the decline in the SAT verbal score between 1963 and 1973 would have been 48 points rather than the actual 35 points had the level of difficulty remained constant. The decline in SAT scores are not the only indication that our schools are in trouble. There have been similarly dramatic declines in other measurements of student achievement: Minnesota Scholastic Aptitude Test, the Iowa Test of Educational Development, and the Comprehensive Test of Basic Skill.

During the period that student achievement was on the decline, per-pupil costs rose from 22 percent to 27 percent of per-capita personal consumption, an indication that the cost of educating children rose at a substantially faster rate than the rate of inflation. Another way of looking at costs: in 1968 the average factory worker worked 218 hours to derive enough gross income to support a child for one year in a public school with average cost, compared with an estimated 282 hours in 1978.

It ought not come as much of a surprise that while costs have escalated and achievement has declined, the public's confidence in its public schools has been waning. Although 48 percent of those questioned in a Gallup poll conducted in 1974 gave the public schools a grade of *A* or *B*, only 37 percent gave those grades in a similar poll conducted in 1977. Whether this decline in confidence has continued on to the present, I do not know, although the figures we have on per-pupil costs and student achievement since 1977 do not suggest that the public has found new reasons to be more approving.

Decline and Fall: Some Nonbargaining Causes

One cannot avoid a certain amount of untidiness when talking about the effect of collective bargaining on educational outcomes. We sometimes attribute to bargaining certain changes in educational performance on the sole ground that the one preceded the other. As Samuel Johnson once observed of physicians, they tended to "mistake subsequence for consequence," opponents of bargaining see the baleful influence of the union in every aspect of declining achievement and increasing costs.

It is not that simple. The figures on achievement and costs are aggregate figures. As far as individual districts are concerned, one does not know whether the extent of unionization is directly related to scores on standardized tests or per-pupil costs. We do know that in 1979 approximately 70 percent of the 2.3 million nonsupervisory instructional staff in the public schools were covered by collective agreements and that there were approximately 10,000 teacher agreements in the nation's 16,000 school districts. Those sections of the country that have the highest degree of unionization, the Northeast and the industrial Midwest, seem also to have suffered the greatest decline in student achievement, but there are no doubt several causes for this decline that are extraneous to bargaining and unionization.

What forces—forces not related to collective bargaining—could be at work to cause a decline in the mastering of verbal and quantitative skills? For one, critics of public education point to the decline in the number and percentage of students taking the more difficult subjects such as physics, advanced mathematics, foreign languages. A lack of rigor has its consequences. One suspects, based on an all-too-casual and superficial look at English instruction in a number of school systems, that not only are fewer students taking advanced courses in English but the content of the remaining courses has become watered down. One does not improve one's facility with the language from reading *Field and Stream* (requiring reading, I am told, in one English course for students who find Browning and Shakespeare not to their taste); nor does one develop many skills in English composition if all examinations are the short-answer type and compositions are not assigned.

There might also be a decline in the quality of recent entrants into the teaching profession, a situation, if true, that must surely have some consequences for student achievement. "Schools of education," writes Timothy Weaver in the September 1979 issue of the *Phi Delta Kappan*, "are now selecting potential educators from among the least academically talented populations applying for admission." The verbal and math SAT scores of these future teachers were well below the average score of college-bound seniors in 1976 (off 34 points in verbal scores and 43 points in math scores). Weaver also reports that according to the National Longitudinal Study sample, education majors, graduating in 1976, ranked fourteenth out of a field of 16 on SAT verbal scores and fifteenth on the math score. Verbal scores were 46 points below the average for graduating seniors; math scores were 52 points below average.

There are other forces that have influenced the way students perform. The mischievous influence of television has been commented upon by too many critics too many times to warrant a discussion here. It suffices only to point out that school children spend an inordinate amount of time before the television set (more time than they do in the classroom), and that television typically does not provide many "mind-stretching" exercises. Indeed, if taken in too heavy doses, TV may render children incapable of engaging in abstract thought. Even such educational and "uplifting" programs as "Sesame Street" seem to have very limited effects on learning. It is possible that television watching can bring youngsters up to first- or second-grade reading levels more quickly than would otherwise be possible, but looking at TV seems to provide few educational benefits beyond that point.

It would not do in an essay such as this to expatiate on the general malaise that seems to have gripped our society. I can only suggest that one manifestation of this malaise is a decline in precision in language usage, a decline that in turn is no doubt reflected in falling SAT verbal scores. If people who are well situated, news commentators, for example, are less than precise in their manner of expression, it should come as no surprise that school children should also be less than precise in their work. Slovenliness in speech and writing is contagious, and if Walter Cronkite, for example, is sometimes confused as to proper syntactic and grammatical construction, that failing can hardly be lost on school children.

Production Functions: The Right Mix for the Best Result

Has collective bargaining added to our educational difficulties? I suggested at the beginning of this essay that I thought that it had, although I remain unsure of the extent of that influence. Neither am I entirely convinced that there is anything intrinsic to the bargaining process that makes a negative influence inevitable. At the moment, however, the effect of bargaining on educational outcomes appears to be on the debit side. In the remainder of this chapter, I will try to point out why I believe this to be so.

It may be, as Coleman, Jencks, and others have told us, that the chief determinant of educational achievement is not the quality of the schools but rather the socioeconomic background of the school child. Still, it is in the schools where most of us learned to read, write, and cipher, and how well the schools teach us these skills depends in large part on how wisely the school's limited resources, economic and human, are allocated. Researchers have recently developed some general ideas as to which kind of expenditures and which teacher characteristics ought to be encouraged if the purpose of education is indeed achievement in the cognitive domain. Even though there are some areas of disagreement among production-function analysts, most tend to agree that there are certain types of school and teacher characteristics that are related to student achievements. Some of the most important will be discussed here.

School characteristics over which school officials have some control, and which seem to be related to student achievement, are as follows: (1) the amount of classroom time students spend with their teachers, that is, the length of the school day and school year. The more time students spend with their teachers, the more they achieve. It follows, then, that any expenditure that would provide for a longer school day and year would, all other matters being equal, be a judicious allocation of scarce resources. (2) Class size: The evidence is mixed on this. Although the more recent studies suggest strongly that a reduction in class size to a level of twenty-five to thirty students is positively associated with the achievement of low achievers, such a reduction would have little influence on the achievement of middle and high achievers. The policy implications of this evidence is that school administrators ought to retain their flexibility in establishing minimum and maximum class size. (3) Support personnel: There is little connection between the amount of psychological and other counseling services afforded to students and the level of student achievement. The policy implications of this "finding" suggests that funds expended in this area might better be used to support the extension of the school day and year and on the selective reduction in class size. (4) Other school characteristics researchers have looked at to determine their relationship to student achievement are the quality of the building principal, extensive use of educational hardware (television, teaching machines, and so on), and the physical condition of school buildings. These studies suggest to us that the quality of the school principal is of critical importance to the achievement of students, although there is little evidence that additional experience or training adds to the principal's quality. Rather, it is that elusive characteristic sometimes referred to as "demandingness" that seems to make the difference. As for the amount of educational hardware used and the quality of the school building, these are matters that seem not to affect student achievement one way or the other. The policy implications of these findings suggest that it would be wise to invest heavily in the selection and nurturing of building principals, but that funds currently being spent on the purchase and maintenance of educational hardware and the construction of fancy new buildings could be more productively spent elsewhere.

As for teacher workforce characteristics that may or may not make a difference, four characteristics production-function analysts have looked at are: verbal ability, teaching experience, graduate education, and maleness. In respect to verbal ability, this may be the most significant teacher characteristic correlated with student achievement, particularly for middle to high student achievers, both at the elementary and secondary level. The single exception is that teachers' high verbal scores seem to have little connection with student achievement in mathematics.

As for experience, there seems to be no direct relationship between the achievement of students and the experience of their teachers. Indeed, as Firman and others have observed, there may even be a negative correlation between the amount of experience teachers have and how well their students achieve. Many teachers evidently begin to "burn out" after fifteen years or so, and that decline in enthusiasm is reflected in the performance of their students. An exception to this correlation is English instruction in the junior and senior high schools. Students at this level appear to develop better verbal skills if they study with more experienced English teachers, all other influences taken into account. Whether English teachers learn to teach better as the years go by, or whether these older teachers are more successful because they are more demanding (they did after all come into the profession when verbal skills and proper English usage were more highly prized) would be an interesting study in itself.

What generally holds for experience also seems to hold for graduate training. Training beyond the baccalaureate is for most teachers usually not associated with student achievement. Although some production-function studies suggest that there is a positive correlation between the percentage of teachers in a district holding the Master's degree and the achievement of students in that district, many analysts have suggested that the MA is merely a proxy for other teacher characteristics (intelligence, drive, imagination) that are more responsible for high student achievement than the training teachers undergo to secure the degree. Indeed, in many studies where there is a control for verbal ability, the effect of the MA is almost washed out.

As for maleness, the evidence is that the more male teachers there are in a district, the lower will be the average student achievement scores. Whether this is because males attracted to the profession are of a lower quality than females or whether the negative relationship between the sex of the teacher and the achievement of pupils has other causes is not known. If it is a question of difference in quality, however, it may be that difference is currently being narrowed. As barriers to female entry into the professions and into business fall, it is likely that many thousands of women who heretofore would have gone into teaching for lack of a better opportunity are now going into such careers as law, medicine, architecture, or business administration. Thus the decline in teaching talent that Timothy Weaver worries about may in some respect be attributed to the increasing fortunes of talented females.

Bargaining, Conditions of Work, and Quality

Now the question is whether the collective-bargaining process prevents resources from being deployed in a fashion that would enhance student achievement. There are of course several school and teacher characteristics that are not subject to change through bargains. One thinks of the socioeconomic background of students, for example, or the quality of the principal, the amount of educational hardware available, or the level and quality of support personnel. Nor has bargaining had much influence on the male-female ratio of the teacher workforce. Approximately 65 percent of public school teachers were female when bargaining began in earnest in the middle of the 1960s, and that percentage was about the same in 1980.

Some school characteristics probably have been affected by bargaining, however, and the two that are most likely to be influenced by a collective agreement are student-teacher contact hours and class size. I pointed out earlier that there appears to be a strong relationship between the amount of time students spend with their teacher and how well students achieve. Many teacher contracts set limits for the length of the school day as well as the number of days of instruction, so long as minimum state requirements are met. A recent study by Charles Perry suggests that bargaining may be responsible for a reduction of 30 to 35 minutes of instruction per school day and that bargaining may also be influencing a trend to keep schools open for only the minimum days allowed by law. This suggests that it was the union and the collective-bargaining process that brought the reduction in teacher-student contact about, that if the employer had been left to his "druthers," there perhaps would have been no reduction, and possibly the number of contact hours would have increased with an accompanying climb in the learning curve.

Maybe so, but this connection between bargaining and the reduction in student contact hours has yet to be demonstrated conclusively. Although it is clearly one of the main objectives of bargaining that the union should get the employer to do things the employer would rather not do, it is less clear that for any given change in the employment arrangement, whether specified in the contract or not, it was the pressure of the union that brought that change about.

There has been a decided change in the pupil-teacher ratio since bargaining began, from a 1965 average of 28 to 1 for elementary schools and 22 to 1 in secondary schools to an average of 23 to 1 elementary and 19 to 1 secondary in 1975. These data, unfortunately, are aggregate data, so one does not know whether improvements in ratios have been more marked in organized districts than in unorganized ones. We do know that a substantial number of collective-bargaining contracts place numerical limits on overall student-teacher ratios and on class size (well over half the contracts in New York State impose some form of limitation), and that indiscriminate limitations may skew resources in a direction not conducive to student achievement. But here again we do not have very persuasive evidence that absent the coercive power of the union, school officials would exercise the kind of discretion in the student-teacher mix that would be best calculated to improve scholastic performance.

The Influence of Bargaining on Teacher Characteristics

To turn to those characteristics of the teacher workforce that may have been affected by bargaining—I suggested earlier that three of the four teacher-characteristics analysts looked at (experience, graduate education, maleness) were not related to student achievement. Verbal ability was the only measurable teacher characteristic that seemed to have a strong positive influence on how well school children achieved. Many students of production-function analysis also point out that there appear to be other teacher characteristics such as a pleasing personality, demandingness, and conscientiousness, that are closely related to achievement. But these characteristics do not lend themselves to easy measurement and are therefore left out of most production-function equations. The percentage of male teachers may also have some influence (downward) on the learning curve, but, as was pointed out earlier, bargaining seems not to have affected either the number or quality of male teachers entering or staying in the profession.

Nor, as Professor Weaver's evidence suggests, has bargaining seemed to have much effect on either the recruitment or retention of teachers, men or women, with high verbal ability. Scholars who have looked at the effect bargaining has had on salaries conclude that the difference in salaries that can be attributed to bargaining is in the 1- to 5-percent range. Moreover, the modest influence bargaining has had on salaries seems to have benefited most those teachers with the greatest amount of experience and graduate training, a development that might give pause to bright and energetic young college graduates who are interested in parlaying their talents into more immediate and more tangible returns.

The effect of bargaining on the recruitment of talented and highly verbal individuals into teaching is an important consideration since one of the main arguments originally advanced in support of bargaining in education was based on the premise that bargaining would cause an increase in salaries that in turn would serve to woo bright young people away from other pursuits and into the schools. Thus bargaining would improve productivity in the schools just as it had in the industrial sector. Many students of bargaining in industry had concluded that bargaining fostered greater industrial efficiency since the wage differential between workers in organized plants and those in unorganized plants (between 10 and 15 percent) allowed for the recruitment of a more productive workforce. The wage bill might be higher for an employer who dealt with a union, but the difference was worth it since the higher paid workers would be more ready to follow instructions, would work harder and smarter, and be less inclined to absenteeism and other forms of industrial mischief.

The effect of bargaining on teacher quality is probably not as great since the 1- to 5-percent effect of bargaining on salaries is probably not sufficient to woo a more qualified group into teacher training and ultimately into the profession. Although it is not possible to calculate what differential would be required in order to produce a significantly more qualified teacher corps, a 5-percent differential (which may prove to be the outer limit of the bargaining effect) is clearly not enough to do the job.

It is perhaps one of the supreme ironies of educational personnel policy that systems of teacher compensation accepted in virtually every district in the country are based on two teacher characteristics that modern scholarship suggests have only a modest relationship to achievement: experience and graduate training. To be sure, teacher unions are not responsible for the complicated and elaborate salary schedules so characteristic of modern teacher-pay schemes. These for the most part emerged during the 1920s and 1930s as a substitute for the chaotic nonsystems that existed up to that time. The point is that just about every school system in the country has a salary scheme that rewards teachers for experience (so many hundred dollars for each year in the system) and for the number of graduate credits or degrees a teacher is able to garner. It is a rare case indeed in which the employers exercise discretion in making salary adjustments because of market forces, the assumption of additional academic responsibilities, or because of superior classroom performance.

The effect of bargaining has been to elevate this archaic system into a matter of high principle. It may make absolutely no sense to distribute scarce resources in this fashion, but to unions, which tend to be both majoritarian and egalitarian, it makes great good sense. The schedule allows for salary payments to be based on purely objective standards. Union leaders are not made to participate in the development of a scheme that would allow for distinctions in salary adjustments based on merit, market forces, or additional duties. The majority of union members would probably benefit far less from any scheme allowing for managerial flexibility in salary matters than they would under a standard schedule, and it is a commonplace occurrence that union leaders will forget only at their peril that when in doubt it is always the majority's interest that must be served.

It is probably for this reason that school administrators, even those familiar with production-function findings and who may wish to have some of these findings implemented, are reluctant to push hard at the bargaining table for greater flexibility in salary arrangements. It is a notion that cannot be sold unless the overall salary adjustment is high and the degree of discretion small. Even then it probably would not be worth the candle.

Another reason for administrators' half-heartedness in the pursuit of flexibility is that few are prepared by temperament, training, or experience to say that teacher A is more worthy than B, or that C is not worthy at all. Administrators' natural timidity on such matters is greatly intensified by the presence of a strong and militant union.

Even in those circumstances where school boards and administrators are eager to "take the union on" on this issue, it is not likely they will succeed. In nearly all instances the issue would go to impasse, and a mediator or a fact finder would be brought in to help resolve the issue. In most instances these neutrals become the ally of the union since most of them, to use the pejorative, are "settlement freaks." A fact finder, say, might believe that the current system of teacher compensation is cruelly irrational, but he also knows that the level of the employer's interest in securing a more rational system is nowhere near the union's level of interest in maintaining the old. He will therefore almost always recommend for the preservation of the old way of doing things, the justification for that decision being couched in language that will speak mainly of the "understandable reluctance of neutrals to plow new ground," of how "preferable it would be for the parties themselves to come to their own agreement" on such a critical issue, of how important it is that neutrals not be put in a position of "substituting their judgment for the judgment of the parties." The reason for this mealy-mouthed approach is that the neutral knows that the union feels more keenly about preserving the status quo than the employer does about changing it, and if settlement is indeed the name of the game, then discretion, if not wisdom and justice, suggests that the recommendations should come closer to the union's position than it does the employer's. One can please the employer and disappoint the union on another issue to even things out.

In the meantime school districts are saddled with salary structures that do not accommodate in any way to what production-function analysts tell us about allocating scarce resources. Premium prices are paid for long experience when the evidence suggests that in most instances long experience is not related to achievement. Districts invest substantial sums in teachers' advanced degrees even though it is clear that there is no student-achievement payoff in such an investment. And at the same time, those who build salary systems refuse to recognize the single teacher characteristic that is related to achievement, verbal ability. It would indeed be difficult to persuade either union leaders or school officials that salary schedules ought to allow for premium pay for those teachers who test high on Graduate Record Exams and other measurements of verbal facility. That such an arrangement is not impossible, however, is shown by certain details of the Burnham Awards, the salary settlement reached between representatives of teachers and of local education authorities covering teachers in England and Wales. There premium pay is given those who graduate from a university as against those who graduate from teacher-training institutions, with an additional premium paid to those who graduate with high honors. From what one can gather, a consequence of these differentials is that at least a sprinkling of highly qualified university graduates who might otherwise have sought employment elsewhere enter the teacher ranks each year, enough to elevate the tone in many local schools. To the extent "university graduates" and "high honors" are proxies for verbal ability, this system of recruiting more talented individuals into teaching works modestly well. The fact that it works at all in egalitarian England ought to give pause to those who worry that our salary arrangements not become contaminated by elitism.

Bargaining in the Schools: What It Might Mean and Portend

Other than those collective-bargaining arrangements covering athletes, musicians, and entertainers, there is a strong tendency toward sameness of treatment in collective-bargaining contracts. It has already been pointed out that both unions and employers find it messy to take superior or inferior performance into account when establishing compensation schedules. Contracts are far easier to negotiate and administer if all matters have been systematized, and all provisions applicable to all employees under all circumstances. This reduction in flexibility so characteristic of bargaining may be contributing in some measure to the decline in achievement. Take, for example, the hours in the school day and the days in the school year. Contracts do not distinguish between the instructional time needed by slow learners and fast learners, between schools in the posh neighborhoods and schools in the ghettos. Thus bargaining seems not only to be responsible for a decline in the total number of hours and days school is kept, it also bears some responsibility for an unproductive uniformity of treatment. Some students and some classes of students require more time with their teachers than do others.

Much the same can be said of class-size provisions. Although some contracts allow for distinctions based on subject matter and student ability, the tendency is to set limits on class size irrespective of the differences in students, subjects, or teaching style. Thus it becomes more difficult to arrange for small classes in those circumstances where small classes are warranted by having these classes "subsidized" by large classes in subject areas where class size is a less important consideration.

I have already discussed the effect of the lock-step system on salary payments characteristic of teacher salary schedules. It need only be pointed out here that the need for uniformity of treatment imposed by bargaining can cause the hard-to-find physics, trigonometry, or home-economics teachers to be paid no more than the dime-a-dozen teachers of social studies or driver education. Thus school districts may be forced to pay above the market price to secure teachers of some subjects while they cannot meet the market price for qualified teachers in other subject-matter areas.

To be sure, no school official is obliged to make concessions or demands affecting the length of the school day or a demand for a uniform reduction of maximum class size. Nor are officials obliged to retain the current compensation system. Indeed, in regard to salary schedules, the current system was imposed long before there was such a thing as collective bargaining; the unions have merely picked up where unilateral authority left off. But there is something about the bargaining process that makes the granting of at least some concessions inevitable. There are few instances indeed when the employer did not give in on some issue. And those concessions tend to be made by the employer; the concessions unions have made—at least until very recently—tend not to result in the relinquishment of rights already won, but rather the reduction or the dropping of a demand. The obligation to reach agreement, the weariness with the process, the possible threat of some form of job action, all these possibilities conspire to cause the employer to make those little accommodations here and there. If neutrals are involved in the bargaining, then one can almost be assured that the employer will make concessions because there can be no end to the impasse unless concessions are forthcoming, and neutrals regard a continuing impasse as they would a particularly loathsome social disease.

One of the hopes many of us held out for teacher bargaining in its early days was that although it might not be possible to directly gauge the positive effect it would have on school output, the improvement bargaining would have on teacher morale would surely have a positive effect on the learning environment. Clearly, teachers would have to feel better about their work if they had the protection of a contract that guarded them from discriminatory treatment, improved working conditions, and gave some assurance that there would be a collective teacher voice in the determination of district policies.

Unfortunately, the evidence on what has happened to teacher morale in recent years does not allow for such a sanguine view. To illustrate, according to recent polls conducted by the NEA, although 78 percent of public school teachers said in 1966 that they would or probably would take up teaching if they had it to do over again, only 63 percent said they were so inclined in 1976. Even more distressing, of those who had reached the "point of no return" age of thirty to thirty-nine, only 57 percent said they would or probably would take up the profession again. Ten years before, 75 percent of this age group said that they were satisfied with their occupational choice. It does not bode well for public education if close to one half of those teachers who have from twenty-five to thirty-five years of service remaining should be voicing regret about their early decision to become teachers. True, as Robert Quinn and Graham Staines have recently reported, there has been a substantial decline in job satisfaction among virtually all occupational groups in recent years. It would be therefore unfair to single out teachers as being the sole victims of a broader social malaise. It does seem to follow, however, that the effect of declining morale on teaching, which is one of the most intimate of occupations, should have graver consequences than would a similar decline in those occupations where there is less reliance on personal relations.

It is possible that the amount of disenchantment would have been more severe had there been no collective bargaining. Surely there is no evidence that bargaining has been the sole or even major cause of this growing disenchantment. But it is just as clear that bargaining has not *improved* morale. Nor, for that matter, has it reduced costs, or led to higher student achievement, or made the public more pleased with the quality of its public schools. None of these goals, of course, were necessarily the goals of collective-bargaining legislation at the time bills were being considered by state legislatures in the 1960s and 1970s. The goal then was to give to a group of citizens (public employees) a right that was enjoyed by others (private employees). It was not argued then that public schools or sanitation services would be better if there was a collective-bargaining law, any more than the framers of the Wagner Act claimed that its passage would result in better Chevies or Plymouths. Those were matters to be taken up at other times in other forums.

Events have not been entirely kind to the proponents of teacher bargaining. Although the growth of the movement has been substantial in terms of the number of teachers covered, number of contracts, and number of states that have passed enabling legislation, the results have not been all that satisfactory. Clearly, bargaining has not brought about a substantial improvement in student achievement. But neither can it be shown that bargaining has in any significant way been responsible for the decline in achievement. Neither can it be said that bargaining has done all that much for teachers, at least as far as salaries are concerned, nor has it had a healthy effect on teacher morale.

This is not to suggest that we will shortly be returning to the status quo ante. Collective bargaining will be the primary method of establishing personnel policies in the schools for the foreseeable future. Indeed, one can predict that within a decade or so we will have enabling legislation in nearly all the twenty or so states that do not currently grant bargaining rights to public employees. Moreover, we will probably see greater liberalization of statutes in those states that already provide for bargaining. Many states that do not at present grant the right to strike will do so, in many jurisdictions the scope of negotiations will be expanded to include issues that have heretofore been deemed to be policy matters, and some form of union security either in the form of union shop, agency shop, or fair-share agreement will be mandated by statute. There is an egalitarian mood abroad in the land, and it will become increasingly difficult for legislatures to resist pressure coming from public employees and their supporters that all distinctions between public and private employment be removed.

There will no doubt be some attempts to counter this trend, but the resistance will be sporadic and isolated. Witness, for example, the rise and fall of a parents' union to combat both the union and the school board in the Philadelphia public schools. Various publics will from time to time become outraged that they are receiving less for more; some will attempt to right the wrongs by demanding greater access to the collective-bargaining process through direct participation, sunshine bargaining, public referendum on the settlement, or some other form of popular influence. The success of such endeavors appear at this date to be problematic.

If we assume that bargaining has had a slightly deleterious effect on quality, and the evidence that it has had any influence one way or the other is more suggestive than anything else, there is still a question as to whether that is a problem endemic to the process. It is true, of course, that the parties to a collective agreement in public education are not disciplined by the market to the extent bargainers in the industrial sector are disciplined. But there is a kind of discipline exercised by a public that is becoming increasingly worried about declining achievement, increasing costs, and the blunting of public influence. It bears remembering that to the public the first order of business is not whether teachers have collective-bargaining rights or are otherwise treated fairly according to some abstract standard. The public's chief concern is that this public enter-prise does an effective job in educating children, uses limited resources effi-ciently, and is responsive to the public will, however that latter term might be defined. Bargaining may have so far had only a modest influence on any of these concerns, but if the public *believes* that bargaining has been a significant cause of our troubles, or at minimum that bargaining contains a real potential for mischief, then political action will be the counterpart to the discipline exercised by the product market in the industrial sector. It would not be the first time that the cure was effective even though the diagnosis was not com-pletely on target.

7 Commentary

John E. Dunlop

Having been closely involved in teacher collective bargaining over the past fifteen years, I read Doherty's chapter with a good deal of interest. I must confess that my initial reaction was primarily one of irritation. Irritation not so much with the fact that Doherty did not offer any good that might have been promoted by bargaining in education but rather irritation with his polemical style. He has developed a new rhetorical twist-damning with very faint criticism. He draws conclusions unfavorable to bargaining from very thin evidence (which he admits to be thin) and then qualifies the conclusions to the point where their usefulness is questionable. But in doing so, he leaves an aftertaste of the criticism pronounced enough to linger on and overwhelm the qualifications. He does this often enough in the chapter to give the reader pause to consider what his fundamental position is on collective bargaining in education. In this regard, I get two distinct impressions from the paper about Doherty's predisposition on this matter. First, I think he believes that collective bargaining is a process unsuited to the operation of the educational enterprise; and second, he really would like to damn it completely.

My irritation aside, I think Doherty has raised some matters that merit extended discussion in a public forum. To begin with, one must keep constantly in mind that collective bargaining is a subsystem that is part of a larger system and that the subsystem is shaped more by the forces at work throughout the larger system than the larger system is shaped by narrow forces of the subsystem. Without such constant reminder, one could easily conclude from reading Doherty's chapter that the opposite were true.

For example, Doherty decries the continued reliance on the uniform salary schedule and argues that a prime ingredient in that continued reliance is collective bargaining. He says in effect that the subsystem governs completely and is unaffected by larger-system factors. I think a fairer approach to understanding the continued reliance on the uniform salary schedule would be to pose the question of whether it would continue to exist today if collective bargaining were not present. I think it would because factors that go to support its continued use exist independent of collective bargaining. For one, any change is unsettling for administrators and teachers, and change that affects a basic concern such as how people are paid is even more unsettling. This disquietude exists in the total system not just in a subsystem of collective bargaining. Such disquietude propels people to act even if it is simply to resist unsettling change. Moreover, unsettling change can be accomplished in any system only when it is clearly demonstrated that the method to be displaced is bankrupt. Clearly this was the case back in the 1920s and 1930s when the uniform salary system replaced the old chaotic system of individual bargaining. Such is not the case today with the uniform salary system. Despite Doherty's criticism, there is significant public-policy good that comes from a system that awards pay on an objective basis. For the most part, people in education are comfortable with it and think it promotes stability and harmony in the workplace. It is a basic principle of compensation theory that the most serious individual employee dissatisfactions that break down morale arise over perceived unjust inequalities in pay. A pay differential based on a factor closely akin to IQ, that is, verbal ability, would in my estimation be perceived as an unjust inequality, for it rewards a trait unaffected by enthusiasm, temperament, training, experience, or a host of other factors deemed important attributes of a prized employee.

Doherty's attachment to a verbal-ability differential, or incentive, illuminates in other ways how larger-system forces are a greater determinant of policies and actions than subsystem forces. Professor Weaver's article referred to by Doherty does not mention collective bargaining. It concerns mainly whether colleges of education are attracting bright students. Doherty extrapolates from the article the need for a verbal-ability differential or incentive concept to attract brighter candidates for teaching. The problem in my estimation is not the lack of a sound, cost-efficient salary policy but rather the lack of a basic resource—money. If bright students are not attracted to teaching, it is because the overall, life-time financial rewards are dismal in comparison to those to be achieved by pursuing careers in engineering, accounting, law, medicine, or the sciences. Tinkering with a verbal-ability incentive system will not change this basic fact. Unless the American public is willing to pay teachers over their life-time career salaries competitive with other professions, the brighter students will not change their minds in any numbers sufficient to effect meaningful changes. The American public has never indicated such willingness before, and there is no reason to believe that changes in the method of salary payments to teachers will alter that disposition. The problem of recruiting bright teachers is a general systemic problem and not a problem attributable even partially to collective bargaining. I suppose Doherty's response to this would be to grant the basic proposition and argue that such circumstance requires a greater concern for the efficient utilization of scarce resources and that the rigidities of collective bargaining blocks implementation of any efficiencies. He seems to indicate that implementation of such efficiencies are required even if the majority of teachers are disadvantaged. For example, he argues that the current method of teacher salary payments "may make absolutely no sense" and then notes that if managers were allowed greater flexibility in salary matters that the majority of teachers ("union members") "would probably benefit far less from any (such) scheme ... than they would under a standard schedule." The only thing I can conclude from all this is that in

Doherty's view the efficiencies gained in benefiting a few through salary incentives based on verbal ability and other factors far outweigh any resulting harm such change will cause through disruption of morale. The implications of this are important to consider, and not as Doherty would have it, because collective bargaining prevents such changes from occurring but that public-policy planners must decide which among competing theories promotes greater efficiency, a task more difficult and trying than one can perceive in Doherty's discussion. Change for efficiency's sake may, in fact, not promote efficiency when all costs are considered. Resistance to change, concern about total payoffs in efficiency resulting from any change, concern about fairness and objectivity in salary payments are motivations alive in the overall system and are not peculiar to a collective-bargaining subsystem nor to unions only.

Turning to Doherty's comments on specific aspects of teacher bargaining, particularly those on student-contact time, class size, and teacher morale, I think generally has admissions of insufficient evidence and the failures of research to demonstrate connections are proper commentaries on the matters he discusses. However, in his zeal to condemn bargaining, he does not provide the kind of qualifications really needed nor does he draw distinctions where warranted. For example, at one point he states, "Bargaining seems . . . to be responsible for a decline in the total number of (teacher-student contact) hours." Although he had stated previously on this matter that "the connection between bargaining and the reduction in student contact hours has yet to be demonstrated conclusively," he still leaves the impression that the connection has been satisfactorily demonstrated in Perry's research and the conclusive connecting up is only a minor matter. Perry's own warnings in the article are, I think, worth noting. Perry first notes that "intensive analysis of the bargaining process and results can only be undertaken in a limited sample of relationships" and then goes on to state that "the obvious weakness in this approach rests in the problem of generalizing any findings, particularly if there is substantial diversity in experience with the sample." Of the nine districts studied, "the length of school year or school day . . . was specified in only five. . . ." Perry concluded that from these five, "there was evidence that collective bargaining contributed to a discernible reduction in hours." To draw conclusions from a study of only nine bargaining situations and apply them to all the thousands of bargaining situations extant in the country today, even attaching the cozy qualifiers "may" and "seem," is in the words of Perry "difficult, if not dangerous."

The Perry article aside, anyone discussing how student contact hours are handled in collective-bargaining agreements should have some impression of the past and current practice in such matters. Traditionally, and collective bargaining has yet to alter practice, teacher hours of work have been opened-ended. In theory, the employer could call on the teacher to perform work at any time from evenings to weekends, and in practice often did. Premium pay being a concept foreign to educators, teachers called on to work beyond the student day received no additional compensation other than their base salary except in limited circumstances such as yearbook advisor and coaching and never in any amount equal to the hours worked. In addition, the workday, workweek, and workyear in education are products more of tradition and interdistrict comparisons than of any other factors. Collective bargaining has not changed to any great extent the employer's ability to call on the teacher to perform uncompensated overtime work, nor the length of the student day, the teacher workweek, or the school year. Collective bargaining has for the most part confirmed existing practices in these matters or merely moved with already existing trends.

In a survey of a sample of teachers on teaching time, covering the period from 1966 to 1976, the NEA found that the number of periods taught by the average teacher and the average length of these periods had not changed in ten years. The average number of student days had declined from 181 to 180 in the same period. Interestingly enough, the Northeast (a heavy bargaining area) was found to have on the average the longest teaching year and the Southeast (a nonbargaining area) the shortest.

Again it is well to keep in mind that the greater determinants of teaching time are factors present in the general system of education and not the factors peculiar to collective bargaining. Tradition and custom are such factors. For example, if, as has been the traditional view, the school year is to be fitted in the time span from the day after Labor Day to mid-June, only so many teaching days are available once traditional holidays and vacation are subtracted. It can be argued that parental resistance to moving school opening to before Labor Day, or school closing to late in June will be as effective as any resistance from a teachers' union to such change.

Finally in regard to student-contact hours, I find it difficult to accept the proposition that increasing teaching time alone will result in higher student achievement. Too many variables are present to allow confidence in such an assertion. The number of students present, student age level, and the total workload of the teachers are factors that must be considered along with added teaching time in assessing the cause of higher student achievement. The simple fact of how well the time available is used may be more crucial to student achievement than the total time spent. In a recent study done in the Baltimore public schools, it was found that students who were actively directed in learning by the teacher for the full period did better than students whose teachers gave them silent work to do for part of the period.

On class size Doherty notes that the tendency in collective-bargaining agreements "is to set limits on class size irrespective of the differences in students, subjects, or teaching style." Such an observation, although probably true, really fails to convey any sense that this topic is one of the most hotly debated in teacher bargaining and that this controversy shapes to a great extent the bargaining results. No other topic creates more argument than proposed limits on class size. Teachers say it is clearly a working condition, school administrators say it is a policy matter solely within their management prerogatives. In addition to the controversy over whether or not it is a mandatory subject of bargaining, controversy is created over the cost of class-size reduction. To reduce the size of classes is an expensive proposition. Given such controversies, the results as manifested in bargaining contracts are predictable. Broad limitations stated as goals or objectives or set sufficiently high to allow for all possibilities are the rule rather than the exception. Usually the only objective achieved is preventing classes from growing larger rather than reducing already overcrowded ones. Teacher proposals that draw fine distinctions on class-size limits are inevitably met with negotiability arguments that consume time and energies. Cost arguments are equally lengthy and difficult. Despite all the problems, however, many teacher unions are making the effort to refine the class-size articles in their collective-bargaining agreements. For example, the Denver Classroom Teachers Association has negotiated a class-size clause that is based on a classification system for all students according to learning disabilities. Such a clause allows for various class-size configurations that are related directly to the needs of the students. Unfortunately, many school administrations would summarily dismiss such a proposal out of hand as being beyond the scope of bargaining.

We now turn to Doherty's views on the collective-bargaining process and how that process fosters or encourages unfavorable results. Of course, I am mindful of Doherty's statement that he "is not entirely convinced there is anything intrinsic in the bargaining process that makes a negative influence inevitable." However, all his subsequent commentary says the opposite. Nowhere is this more obvious than in his discussion of the role of neutrals in resolving impasses. After characterizing school administrators as being naturally timid, he intimates that only the rare strong school board and administration would be eager to take a union on over matters they hold dear. He then argues that given certain facets of the collective-bargaining process, in particular impasse resolution machinery, "it is not likely they will succeed." To Doherty, neutrals (mediators and fact finders) are warped by their desire to achieve settlement. He argues that unions are less malleable on the tough issues than are management representatives, that the neutrals know this, and therefore neutrals will always gravitate toward the union positions. This is all very neat and very simple, but it really does not accurately characterize the dynamics of the settlement process where neutrals are concerned.

First of all, mediators are definitely settlement oriented and will try to determine which side is the weaker party, hoping thereby to pressure that party into settlement. But it is not always the union that is the stronger party even where drastic changes are being urged. Moreover, even in mediated settlements involving the abandonment of dearly held management positions, especially ones calling for significant changes, management may have concluded independent of any mediator urgings that the effort to make the change and its resulting costs in terms of teacher morale and labor harmony are not worthwhile.

Fact finders are supposed to function differently than mediators and for that reason are probably not settlement minded in the same way as mediators. Fact finders are suppose to look at, among other things, the equities in bargaining disputes and make recommendations accordingly. Because a fact finder recommends against a management position does not mean ipso facto that the union felt "more keenly about preserving the status quo than the employer (did) about changing it." Take for instance Doherty's favorite issue, the salary schedule. I can say with some confidence that no fact finder in the country (Doherty excepted) would find the current system of teacher compensation "cruelly irrational." It is neither cruel nor irrational. A teachers' union in fact finding can demonstrate its fairness, objectivity, and rationality, and the management counterclaims, however brilliant, will not destroy them. The fact finder is then left to choose, and his choice may not be on what Professor Doherty labels "mealy-mouthed" principles but rather on the age-old precept that he who proposes change carries the burden of demonstrating its worth. In adversary proceedings, it is called the burden of persuasion, and where salary-schedule matters are concerned, such burden is heavy, and a fact finder will be persuaded to change the status quo only after, all things considered, he is convinced that the good to be achieved far outweighs the bad. The current production analyses do not provide school administrators with that sort of convincing proof.

Finally we come to Doherty's views on the influence, or noninfluence, collective bargaining has had on teacher morale. He argues in effect that because over the intervening years teacher morale has declined, collective bargaining could not have contributed to its improvement; therefore collective bargaining is to be faulted. I am sure a logician could find a flaw in this argument. Even if it is not flawed on logical grounds, he states only part of the case. A result of collective bargaining has been the adjudication of day-to-day personnel disputes through grievance arbitration. By NEA estimates these run to almost 10,000 a year. In reading these arbitration decisions, one cannot help being struck by the fact that teachers on many matters affecting their daily professional lives are getting fair hearings and fair rulings. School boards that promise sabbatical leaves and then deny them summarily for reasons of "financial exigency" have been found to violate teacher rights. The same holds true with disputes involving evaluations, sick leave, class size, dismissals, preparation periods, and many other subjects that are at the heart of the average teacher's employment. I am convinced teacher morale is favorably affected by these decisions although I have yet to read a scholarly analysis of such effect. Even when teachers lose their claims in arbitration, they have a greater sense of being treated fairly than when denied the same claim unilaterally by a board of education. The point is that teacher morale can be affected by many aspects of teacher bargaining, and a blanket conclusion "that bargaining has not improved morale" is simply not warranted.

Doherty began his conclusion by saying that "events have not been entirely kind to proponents of teacher bargaining." I would add events over the past fifteen years have not been kind to any beginning movement that is intimately involved in matters directly relating to the U.S. economy. Consumer-protection and ecological concerns are two other movements being buffeted by the winds of economic misfortune, and such buffeting does not make them any less worthy. He then goes on to note that the public's chief concern is that public education "does an effective job in educating children," and "not whether teachers have bargaining rights or are otherwise treated fairly." He concludes by saying that if the public perceives bargaining to be a significant cause of trouble or even a real potential for mischief, it will act politically to effect a cure. I agree, but have a different kind of faith in the American public than I sense Doherty has. Changes will come only after full public debate and will not be the products of ill-tempered pique or misconceived notions of cause and effect. As a matter of fact, such debate is going on right now, and the fact that no one is seriously proposing to abandon the system of collective bargaining in education where it exists now underscores its basic utility as a valid public policy. For the good of the system, in other words, its value to the general system of education lies in the simple fact that it limits conflict and in all the ways it limits conflict, from exclusive recognition (limiting the parties to the conflict), to the scope of bargaining (limiting the subjects of conflict), through the collective agreement (limiting conflict in time), and beyond, it serves to promote the public interest of stability and harmony in the workplace, factors that directly affect the education of children and the efficient use of limited resources.

8   Commentary

R. Theodore Clark, Jr.

Public-sector collective bargaining became a fact of life rather than a mere curiosity in the 1960s. Led by Wisconsin's historic enactment of a mandatory bargaining law covering municipalities and school boards in 1959 and President Kennedy's issuance of Executive Order 10988 in 1962, a virtual onslaught of public-sector legislation was enacted in the 1960s. This trend continued into the 1970s, albeit at a slower pace during the last half of the decade. Today thirty-one states have compulsory collective-bargaining laws covering teachers and other certified instructional personnel. Moreover, in states like Illinois and Ohio that do not have such laws, a substantial number of school districts engage in collective bargaining with their certificated personnel.

While approximately 50 percent of all public employees belong to unions or employee organizations, nearly 75 percent of all teachers belong to such organizations. Except for fire fighters, teachers are the most highly organized group of public employees in the United States. Of the 27,418 collective-bargaining agreements negotiated by public bodies in effect as of October 1976, more than 50 percent—14,072—were entered into by school districts.

The introduction of collective bargaining in the public sector in the 1960s was accompanied by high hopes and great expectations. For example, the report of the task force appointed by President Kennedy that recommended the extension of limited bargaining rights to federal employees stated that "responsible employee organizations can contribute substantially to the efficiency and effectiveness of public services" and that the need for a labor-management policy at the federal level should not be viewed as "a challenge to be met so much as an opportunity to be embraced." Similar hopes were frequently expressed at the state and local level as well.

It has now been twenty years since the historic first collective-bargaining agreement between the New York City Board of Education and the United Federation of Teachers. It is most appropriate that Doherty, with his unique and impressive credentials, has undertaken the important task of attempting to ascertain the impact of collective bargaining on educational "outputs" and whether the high hopes and expectations that accompanied the introduction of collective bargaining in public education have been fulfilled. As Doherty notes, the lack of hard statistical documentation makes this task difficult. This inability to document with finite preciseness, however, should not deter efforts to assess and gauge the impact.

85

My views and opinions are very much the product of my own experience. For the past fifteen years I have represented dozens of boards in negotiations with teacher unions, negotiated scores of contracts with other public and private employers, written extensively on various facets of public-sector collective bargaining, participated on various study commissions, taught courses and seminars on public-sector collective bargaining, and written extensively on the subject. While I too lack the hard documentation that Doherty alludes to, I have developed some definite thoughts and observations with respect to the impact of collective bargaining on public education.

That collective bargaining has had an impact on educational outputs seems clear. Moreover, while I am familiar with a few situations in which collective bargaining has resulted in more pluses than minuses, I would agree with Doherty that the impact in general has been more negative than positive. My reasons for so concluding are somewhat different and, on occasion, at variance with the reasons suggested by Doherty.

Doherty notes that there is a positive correlation between student-teacher contact hours and student achievement. Nevertheless, Doherty notes that the "connection between bargaining and the reduction in student contact hours has yet to be demonstrated conclusively." While I do not have the solid documentation that Doherty is looking for, I do know that collective bargaining has resulted in substantial pressures to reduce the minutes of instruction per day and the number of pupil attendance days per year. Based on my own experience, I know that the number of pupil attendance days in many districts has been reduced as a result of negotiations to the minimum number specified by state law. Moreover, this downward adjustment would not have been made if the school board had been left to its "druthers."

The amount of student-teacher contact hours is also directly affected by the amount of paid time off that teachers are eligible to receive. Rare indeed is the public education negotiation in which the teachers' union does not seek additional paid time off for such reasons as personal-leave days, sick-leave days, professional leave, and union activities. Because collective bargaining does, as Doherty notes, "conspire to cause the employer to make . . . little accommodations here and there," increased paid time off has been negotiated in a substantial number of board-teacher collective-bargaining agreements, especially when viewed over the span of the past ten to fifteen years.

The typical union response is that such additional paid time off does not result in any decrease in the number of student-teacher contact hours because substitutes will be employed to fill in for teachers on paid leave. While this may be accurate in a quantitative sense, it is highly misleading in a qualitative sense. Every study that I have seen demonstrates that a positive learning environment is not fostered and enhanced by the frequent use of substitute teachers. These same studies show that no real learning generally takes place on the day or days when a substitute is in the classroom. This is not to downgrade the valiant efforts of substitute teachers; rather, it is a recognition of the fact that it is impossible to expect substitute teachers, often on short notice, to fill in for a day or two and provide the same level of instruction that the regular teacher would have provided. This is simply not possible.

Doherty notes that many studies have concluded that "the quality of the school principal is of critical importance to the achievement of students." I agree. Doherty, however, dismisses the impact of collective bargaining on the quality of school principals, stating that it is "not subject to change through bargains." While this may have some validity in a literal sense, I would strongly disagree with the conclusion that collective bargaining has not had an impact on the quality of principals.

Prior to the advent of collective bargaining in public education, the building principal was, in a very real sense, the final authority with respect to the day-to-day operation of his or her building. With collective bargaining, however, there has been a very real loss of authority by building principals. Matters that used to be settled at the building level by the principal are now settled by the board in direct negotiations with the teachers union, often without any direct input from the principal. Moreover, most collective-bargaining agreements covering teachers contain grievance procedures that terminate in binding arbitration. This means that teachers now have the contractual right to challenge the decisions of principals and to appeal such matters to the central-office level and, failing resolution, to take the matter to binding arbitration. Rather than having the final say, the principal is now frequently caught in the middle of the adversarial battle between the teachers on the one hand and central-office administrators and the board on the other. To suggest that this has made the job of being a principal less attractive merely states the obvious.

Doherty notes that "demandingness" is the characteristic that results in a principal's positive influence on student achievement. Yet this very quality is subject to compromise and limitation by virtue of the various provisions contained in a collective-bargaining agreement. In other words, even if a school principal possesses "demandingness," it may be difficult for the principal to successfully assert it. And if a principal is bold enough to demand more of his or her staff, a grievance may well be submitted challenging the action.

Collective bargaining has also had an impact on principals in monetary terms. While studies suggest, as Doherty notes, that collective bargaining has only increased teachers' salaries in the 1- to 5-percent range, collective bargaining in many districts has had a major impact on the percentage of a district's budget that is allocated for teachers' salaries and fringe benefits. It is not at all unusual to find that there has been a substantial increase in the percentage of the budget allocated for teacher salaries and fringe benefits between 1960 and 1980. What this means is that there are fewer dollars, computed as a percentage of the budget, available for other purposes, whether it be for administrative salaries, educational supplies, extracurricular activities, or capital expenditures. Not infrequently teachers have been able to negotiate their increased share of the economic pie to the positive disadvantage of building principals and middle-level administrators. Unfortunately, many school boards have a tendency to economize and pinch pennies at the expense of those who are not covered by the negotiations process.

The net result is that in many districts collective bargaining for teachers has made the principal's job more difficult, stifled the principal's ability to initiate action, and adversely affected compensation. Is it any wonder that some principals and school administrators have turned in self-defense to collective bargaining? In Minneapolis and Philadelphia, to cite but two examples, principals are represented by the Teamsters Union. And in 1976 the AFL-CIO issued a charter to the American Federation of School Administrators and Supervisors.

Nearly all salary schedules in public education grant step increases based on years of experience, with lane changes based on the accumulation of additional graduate credits and/or degrees. Yet, as Doherty observes, studies suggest that experience and additional graduate credits "have only a modest relationship to achievement." Salary schedules that treat every teacher exactly the same create no real incentive to excel. Moreover, such salary schedules assume that it is just as easy to employ a special-education teacher as it is a social-studies teacher, but the realities of the labor market increasingly demonstrate the fallacy of this assumption. This has to have a very real impact on the quality of the individuals employed in the hard-to-fill positions.

While collective bargaining, as Doherty noted, is not the progenitor of lock-step salary schedules, collective bargaining makes it very difficult to negotiate salaries that are based at least in part on merit and performance rather than entirely on the passage of time and the accumulation of credits and degrees. In a recent study released by the Illinois State Board of Education of the teacher salary practices in the state's 1100 school districts, only 25 mostly smaller districts had adopted a salary program based on merit or performance evaluation of individual teachers. I would fully agree with Doherty that the existence of lock-step salary schedules "might give pause to bright and energetic young college graduates who are interested in parlaying their talents into more immediate and more tangible rewards."

I would take issue with Doherty's comment that "bargaining seems not to have affected either the number or quality of new teachers entering or staying in the profession." Doherty notes that studies show that the effect of bargaining on salaries is only in the "1- to 5-percent range," suggesting that this is not sufficient to attract and retain quality teachers. This analysis, however, only examines one half of the equation. It is also necessary to inquire whether collective bargaining in public education has been a "turn off," that is, whether collective bargaining has had a negative impact on the recruitment and retention of quality teachers.

My own conclusion, based on numerous conversations with teachers, former teachers, and administrators is that the existence of collective bargaining in public education has tended to be a turn off among those that are most qualified. Teaching is a profession, and professional employees, at least in this country, tend not to desire unionization unless it is necessary for defensive reasons. It should come as no big surprise then that many teachers and would-be teachers embrace collective bargaining with less than total enthusiasm. Moreover, the highly adversarial nature of collective bargaining in public education, including strikes, picketing, and name calling, is hardly designed to enhance the reputation or attractiveness of the teaching profession. As a result, many of the more qualified are seeking other careers, especially in today's labor market in which both men and women have access to other professions and careers.

I should note that collective bargaining is not the *sole* reason why many qualified individuals who might have gone into teaching in the past are now choosing other professions or careers. Certainly, as Doherty observes, the elimination of barriers to female entry into the professions and the business world means that many women who would have previously gone into teaching are now pursuing careers in other professions. Moreover, the many demands that society places on public education probably makes teaching less attractive today than it was twenty-five years ago. Despite these other factors, it would nevertheless be a mistake to believe that collective bargaining has not also been a contributing factor.

There are at least four ways in which collective bargaining has had an impact on student achievement that were not mentioned by Doherty that I believe warrant discussion and consideration. First, the delivery of educational services, which requires a close working relationship between administrators and teachers, tends to be jeopardized by the process of negotiations. I never cease to be amazed by the amount of mistrust exhibited and felt by both administrators and teachers toward each other during negotiations. This mistrust not infrequently results in a situation where there is, in effect, an invisible shield between administrators on the one hand and teachers on the other during the bargaining process, especially when the parties approach an impasse situation. This in turn leads to a breakdown in the cooperation and communications that are necessary to deliver high-quality educational services. It is almost as if both sides feel that it would be a sign of weakness to attempt to cooperate at a point in time when the parties are engaged in an adversarial battle. The problems flowing from this phenomenon are aggravated by the fact that the negotiations process typically last six months or longer and is frequently done on an annual basis. Where this is the case, the parties are almost continually in an adversarial position vis-à-vis each other.

Second, Doherty does not comment on the impact of strikes on student achievement. In 1958 there were only 15 public-sector strikes, and none involved teachers. In 1977 there were 413 strikes, of which 138 involved teachers. Teacher strikes, and especially long strikes, disrupt the continuity of instruction and not infrequently result in lost days of instruction, that is, instruction days that are not made up after the end of the strike. Since there is a positive correlation between the amount of time teachers spend with students and student achievement, the disruption and loss of time due to strikes must on balance have a negative impact on student achievement.

There is another impact caused by teacher strikes that has not received the attention that it should. Most teacher strikes are preceded by an escalating campaign by the teacher union to build solidarity and support for the strike. Thus it is not unusual for strike committees to be activated and actively functioning prior to the start of negotiations. In recent years, many teacher organizations have adopted campaign slogans, accompanied with buttons, literature, rallies, and so on. Since this activity often extends over several months, it seems obvious that it detracts from the primary responsibility of teachers to instruct their pupils.

A strike or threatened strike also involves a psychological tug of war that extracts its costs on those who are affected by it. In order to assure success in any strike situation, teacher unions increasingly resort to pressures of various kinds, some subtle and some not. For teachers who do not desire to strike, these pressures can become very intense. While teacher unions would like to refer to these efforts as friendly persuasion, in many instances they are anything but friendly persuasion.

The impact of teacher strikes on the delivery of educational services is clearly suggested by the following questions posed by Rev. Jesse Jackson:

> How clear is their right to strike if a preoccupation with guaranteed employment usurps the objective of guaranteeing education?
>
> How clear is the right to strike when a union seeks contract protection for incompetence, and so undercuts the competent?
>
> How clear is the right to strike for more money when the employer—a taxpaying parent—holds tax receipts in one hand and test results in the other that prove he's paying more and more for less and less?
>
> And how clear is the right to strike when the union doesn't calculate what it will cost a child whose teacher walked out of the classroom?"[1]

Third, the cultivation and establishment of a trade-union mind-set on the part of bargaining-unit members tends, in my view, to have an adverse impact on student achievement. In years past the teacher who put forth extra effort, stayed late to tutor students, sponsored extracurricular activities, attended open houses, and so on, was respected for his or her extra effort. With the establishment of a union mind-set in some districts, pressure is increasingly brought to bear on the teacher who gives such extra effort. Thus efforts are not infrequently made to discourage the performance of such extra tasks on the ground that it makes other bargaining-unit members look bad by comparison. In the private sector, craft unions have established production quotas and, with the Supreme Court's approval, have even fined employees for exceeding the quota established by the union. While production quotas as such have not found their way into public education, the idea that one should not do more than the others so as to make the others look bad has.

Fourth, collective bargaining has probably had an adverse impact on another determinant of student achievement noted by many researchers, that is, the extent and degree of parental involvement. As a result of collective bargaining, many contracts now contain limitations on the number of parent-teacher meetings and/or open houses that a teacher must attend or make such attendance voluntary. For example, the contract between the Chicago Board of Education and the Chicago Teachers Union provides that "the Union agrees to urge its members to continue to participate in one open house during each school year, whether held during or after school hours." Translated, this means that attendance at an open house is voluntary and that the union will encourage its members only to voluntarily attend one such open house each year. Moreover, many parents seek to talk to their children's teachers prior to or at the end of the pupil instruction day. However, there has been considerable pressure as a result of collective bargaining to shorten or eliminate the period of time a teacher is required to be in school prior to the start of or after the end of the pupil instruction day. Of course, such provisions further limit the opportunities parents have to discuss school-related problems with their children's teachers. I do not question the fact that there are many teachers who continue to make arrangements to meet with parents on their own time despite the existence of such contractual provisions. My point is that the existence of such provisions tends to limit the availability of teachers to engage in meaningful dialogue with the parents of their students.

The decline in student achievement at a time when per-pupil costs are climbing at a substantially faster rate than the rate of inflation suggests that some changes in public education may well be needed. It is appropriate then to examine what impact, if any, collective bargaining will have on the ability of public education to implement change.

Although I would like to believe otherwise, I am forced to conclude that collective bargaining will on balance make change more difficult. Unions are by their very nature status quo oriented, and teacher unions are no exception. As John Gardner noted in his book *Self-Renewal: The Individual and the Innovative Society*:

> Every manager of a large-scale enterprise knows the difference between the kinds of organizational commitment that limit freedom of action and the kinds that permit flexibility and easy changes of direction. But few understand how essential that flexibility is for continuous renewal. . . .

In colleges and universities many of the regulations regarding required courses which are defended on highly intellectual grounds are also powerfully buttressed by the career interests of the faculty members involved in those courses. . . . In the labor movement make-work rules, featherbedding, excessively strict seniority provisions and the closed shop all respresent arrangements that are the crystalization of vested interests.

It is not my purpose here to make the point that such vested interests exist: that point has frequently been made. It is my purpose to point out that they are among the most powerful forces producing rigidity and diminishing capacity for change. And these are the diseases of which organizations and societies die.

Also pertinent is the observation of the Carnegie Commission on Higher Education in its final report that among the forces "lined up against reform" in higher education is "[t]he advent of collective bargaining with its emphasis on formal rules and policies, and its purpose of protecting established faculty interests." In my judgment, this observation is equally applicable to elementary and secondary education.

I agree with Doherty that collective bargaining will be the primary method for determining the salaries and fringe benefits of teachers in the forseeable future. The mere fact that collective bargaining, in my judgment, has had more of a negative than positive impact on the output of educational services does not mean that collective bargaining will be any less of a force tomorrow than it is today. Given this reality, and as a supporter of collective bargaining where a majority of the nonsupervisory employees in an appropriate bargaining unit desire to engage in the process, I do have a number of recommendations on how collective bargaining in public education can be improved in order to minimize the adverse impacts and to accentuate its positive aspects.

First, there is a need on both sides of the bargaining table to lower the level of invective that is frequently part of the bargaining process in public education today. While such invective may win a battle in a given negotiations, it may well aid in losing the war in attempting to regain the public's confidence in the ability of public schools to provide quality educational services. Without the public's support, it will be increasingly difficult to obtain the necessary funding to support both salaries and programs.

Second, in order to eliminate the "guaranteed annual argument" and all the attendant problems with the delivery of educational services, school boards and teacher unions should attempt to negotiate multiyear agreements. Moreover, there is no reason why the period for negotiations has to be six or nine months rather than the sixty-day period that is customary in the private sector.

Third, there is a need to provide some flexibility in teachers' salary schedules that would give some recognition to performance and to what is needed in order to attract and retain qualified teachers in hard-to-fill positions.

It is to the benefit of neither party to go along with a lock-step salary schedule that prevents rewarding exceptional performance and makes it difficult to employ a qualified trigonometry or physics teacher.

Fourth, there is a need to break away from the trade-union mentality that demands uniformity and solidarity at literally any price. While perhaps understandable from a narrow organizational standpoint, it is difficult to defend in the context of public education. Diversity rather than sameness should be encouraged by administrators and teacher unions alike.

Fifth, the important role played by school principals should be given proper recognition in terms of their salaries and fringe benefits. School principals should not be forced to take what is left after negotiations with the teachers. They are entitled to at least equal consideration with the teachers in terms of adjustments to salaries and fringe benefits.

Note

1. Jesse Jackson, "Teacher Strikes and Moral Reaction." Reprinted in a report of the committee on Economic Development, "Improving Management of the Public Work Force: The Challenge of State and Local Government, 1978.

Commentary

Peter E. Obermeyer

Doherty's statement concerning the impact of teacher-school-board collective bargaining on education generally and student achievement particularly identifies significant issues for education, labor, management, and the public. My response will center primarily on those areas where I disagree with his statements or where additional comment is necessary. The statement is a descriptive and accurate discussion of the effect collective bargaining has on education and develops the concept of "product functions." The article refines the pioneering "product function" work done by Heim and Perl.[1]

This response will be organized in five parts dealing with the major issues that were raised. The issues discussed will be as follows:

1. The state of education
2. Impact of collective bargaining on school characteristics
3. Impact of collective bargaining on teacher characteristics
4. The mediator and teacher-school-board collective bargaining
5. Concluding thoughts on education and collective bargaining

The public's attitude toward, or judgment of, public education and those responsible for it is no better or worse than the public's judgment of other segments or institutions of American society. Collective bargaining, government, university professors, health care, mediators, roads, and attorneys are all viewed with some sourness and concern by the public.[2] There exists a feeling of frustration and concern about society generally as well as its major elements. We should, however, keep in mind the public's general concern and confusion with most of our institutions and professions. This contemporary public attitude should serve as a challenge to identify and correct valid concerns and criticisms of education.

In considering contemporary public education, I am struck by its extremes. At one extreme, I am totally impressed with the depth of knowledge, the scope of subjects, and the intensity of learning that some students display and some teachers instill. At the other extreme, I am disappointed at the seemingly putting-in-time attitude of some students. This of course is the paradox into which this series of articles will in some small way attempt to provide insight.

Impact of Collective Bargaining on School Characteristics

Doherty suggests that there are several school characteristics that have been identified and investigated to determine their impact on student achievement. Two of these characteristics, student-teacher contact hours and class size, have been influenced by collective bargaining. I would suggest that a third school characteristic, the quality and effectiveness of the building principal, has also been significantly affected.

Student-Teacher Contact

The amount of time teachers spend in direct classroom contact with students has been reduced by collective bargaining in three primary ways: a reduction of the workday, a reduction of the workyear, and an increase in the number and kind of valid paid absences from work. If the amount of student-teacher contact time affects student achievement, it can be concluded that collective bargaining therefore has reduced student achievement.[3]

An analysis of teacher–school-board collective-bargaining contracts does demonstrate that the process has at least *specifically established* the maximum workday, the maximum workyear, and the number and kinds of paid absences for teachers. It may not be all that clear that collective bargaining has in fact *reduced* the workday and workyear or *increased* the number or kinds of paid absences. Some will argue that collective bargaining has only established in written-contract form these terms and conditions that previously varied from teacher to teacher, building to building, or school year to school year. For many teachers this in itself is justification enough for choosing collective bargaining.

Collective bargaining has affected the workday by specifically defining the maximum number of hours of work per day, the maximum amount (as class periods, minutes, or hours) of student contact per day, the establishment of paid duty-free lunch periods, and the minimum amount (as class periods hours, or minutes) of daily preparation time.

The impact of collective bargaining on the workyear is similar to its influence on the workday. Although the total number of alleged workdays established by a contract may vary because of the reference to student days, workshop days, parent-teacher days, vacations, or holidays, the ultimate standard is how many days the teacher is obligated to be at work. The trend is unmistakable, fewer days. The question remains, however, without bargaining, would a similar trend have occurred? As Doherty points out, "Although it is clearly one of the main objectives of bargaining that the union should get the employer to do things the employer would rather not do, it is less clear that for any given change in the employment arrangement, whether specified in the contract or not, it was the pressure of the union that brought that change about."

The increase in the number of circumstances for which a teacher can be absent from work without loss of pay does not directly reduce the amount of student-teacher contact time because of the use of substitute teachers. Such absences must, it would seem, influence the continuity and effectiveness of the normal teaching relationship. The array of paid absences in the form of sick leave, personal leave, funeral leave, family-illness leave, and union-activity leave, no matter how justifiable, does reduce the amount of time the regular teacher spends in student-teacher contact.

Class Size

Although I am still convinced that the evidence in regard to class size and student achievement is mixed, the issue of class size does affect teachers and teacher unions in two obvious ways. First, given reasonably similar students, teaching a smaller number of students is easier, or at least less demanding, than teaching a larger number. Whatever the impact on student achievement may or may not be, an improvement in the work environment (reduction of class size) is an understandable union-bargaining objective. And second, although the reduction of class size often has a direct relationship to the cost of the settlement—more teachers to spread available settlement dollars among—it does meet a traditional union-bargaining objective of saving jobs and expanding membership work opportunities.

Building Management

Doherty states that "the quality of the school principal is of critical importance to the achievement of students." Even though they are normally not covered by teacher-school-board collective-bargaining contracts, collective bargaining has brought to public education an increasing recognition of the role of the building principal as a manager in its truest sense. The term "educational leader" no longer fits the realities that collective bargaining has placed on the building principal. The role of "manager" must be emphasized because of the importance it has in allocating and accounting for the various "production functions" assigned to the individual building. I would conclude that teacher-school-board collective bargaining has and will continue to demand of building principals a commitment to those management skills absolutely necessary in a highly labor-intensive organization.

If collective bargaining has done nothing else for public education, it has identified the role and need for managers as building principals. It is, as Doherty has concluded, the one "school characteristic" that significantly affects student achievement.

The policy implications of these findings suggest that it would be wise to invest heavily in the selection and nurturing of building principals.

Impact of Collective Bargaining on Teacher Characteristics

Of the four teacher characteristics seriously researched (experience, graduate education, maleness, and verbal ability), only the verbal ability of the teacher has any measurable impact on student achievement. Teacher–school-board collective bargaining promotes a system of salary compensation that does not encourage, and perhaps retards, the one teacher characteristic that does enhance student achievement. Doherty concluded that:

It is perhaps one of the supreme ironies of educational personnel policy that systems of teacher compensation accepted in virtually every district in the country are based on two teacher characteristics that modern scholarship suggests have only a modest relationship to achievement experience and graduate training.

It is frustrating to know that there are superior teachers, as there are superior mediators, lawyers, and deans, that cannot apparently be identified. Even if such superior teachers could be identified, they would be paid based on a salary system that is based on experience and educational attainment. Certainly a system of compensation cannot be developed that is based solely on contemporary research or on the single identifiable teacher characteristic resulting in student achievement. There does seem therefore to be significant reason to direct research toward identifying or isolating those characteristics that produced student achievement. If a "pleasing personality, damandingness, or conscientiousness, . . ." or if class size, good management, hot lunches, or 52-week school years improve student achievement, our obligation should be to identify those characteristics that do affect student achievement and those that do not. Given the dollars that are committed to educational research (which are overwhelming in comparison to the dollars committed to researching collective bargaining), there is a serious need to direct current educational research to identifying these elusive characteristics. Whether collective bargaining can produce a contract that supports or encourages those characteristics is a separate question. But at least the parties should have the benefit of understanding those characteristics that do influence student achievement.

Collective bargaining in education has produced contract standards that directly affect the ability of the industry to attract and retain personnel. The concern of course is *who* is attracted and *who* is retained. Unfortunately, it remains virtually impossible to identify which teachers significantly improve student achievement. Given the current supply-and-demand situation that exists in public education, there are three characteristics of collective-bargaining contracts that significantly influence the ability of the industry to attract and retain teachers: salary-schedule impact, layoff procedures and early-retirement programs.

Salary-Schedule Impact

The teacher salary schedule is a system of compensation that is based on years of experience and the amount of education. Its fundamental characteristics encourage *persistence* in that a person entering the profession will be financially rewarded by staying for a period of ten to fifteen years and achieving additional training. This system is effective provided an employee can accept a relatively low starting salary in exchange for a predictable system of increases over a period of time based on length of service and additional educational attainment. The salary schedule that results from collective bargaining is a means, not withstanding the "professional" intentions of teacher unions, of distributing available settlement dollars to those who are employed at the time of settlement. The obligation of a labor union is to effectively satisfy the demands of employees it represents at *the time of settlement*, not those who may be employed in the future. Therefore the resulting salary schedule may very well produce a starting level of compensation that will attract to the profession only the most dedicated. Practically the starting salaries of the negotiated schedule become the "problem" of the employer. The relatively low starting salary may be acceptable during periods of labor abundance; however, it quickly becomes intolerable during periods of general or specific subject-area labor shortages.

Layoff Procedures

As is true in America's private sector, collective bargaining between teachers and school boards has resulted in a layoff procedure that is based on seniority provided licensing or certification standards are met. Such a system is relatively easy to administer provided there is a clear and understandable definition of seniority and what its uses are. Layoff by seniority does not necessarily reflect a system that retains teachers having an influence on student achievement, but it is a reflection of the system found acceptable in both the private and public sectors.

Although efficient, a layoff system based on the last-hired-first-fired benchmark does not provide an environment of stability for new entrants to the labor market particularly during periods of labor surpluses and declining student enrollments. The result of a layoff becomes more complex when the cost of a teacher is added to the reduction of staff process. Assuming that most layoffs are motivated to some degree by economics, either dropping enrollments or limited revenues, layoffs based on seniority involve "cheaper" teachers rather than "expensive" teachers. In effect, nearly twice as many low-seniority-low-salary schedule placement–low-cost teachers must be eliminated to equal the same cost as high-seniority-high-salary schedule placement–high-cost teachers.

Early-Retirement Programs

As a reaction to the labor-supply imbalance currently existing and a desire to replace high-cost teachers, an intricate series of early-retirement incentive benefits are being negotiated. These incentives are manifested by cash payoffs based on unused sick leave and years of experience, continued participation in group-insurance programs, long-term unpaid leaves of absence to allow for the development of a second career, and part-time teaching arrangements. All these incentives have as their basis the encouragement of teachers with extensive experience and education to retire from the profession. The financial impact is significant. Teachers with experience, which places them at the top of the salary schedule, and the attainment of a masters degree or beyond "cost" two to two and one-half times as much as a first-year B.A. teacher. Whether there is or is not an educational advantage to early retirement, the *economic* savings is significant.

The ability of public education to retain personnel is fundamentally a reflection of each individual teacher's placement or location on the salary schedule. Teachers with little experience and advanced training are faced with the distinct possibilities of layoff and a relatively low salary. Practically, teachers entering the labor market with advanced degrees (M.A. or doctorate) may find their employment opportunities severely limited because of their cost to the employer. In effect, a teacher entering the market should have no more than a B.A. degree prior to employment; and once having found employment, and only then, make the commitment to earning advanced degrees. Teachers in the middle two thirds of the salary schedule will be subject to limited possibilities of layoff and relatively large increases. The increases would result from the general salary-schedule increase, the experience step increase, and the possibility of education lane advancement. Those teachers on the maximum of the salary schedule in terms of experience and additional qualifying training will have permanency of employment but will be subject to minimal salary increases. These teachers who will generally be in the highly productive ages of thirty-five to fifty-five will face the options of (1) remaining committed, challenged, or dedicated to the profession, (2) remaining in the profession only because there is no career alternative or, (3) attempting to directly influence the outcome of collective bargaining to provide additional dollars for senior employees.

Given current and short-run economic realities (limited hiring at best and extensive layoffs at worst), the number of highly experience teachers will increase significantly. These teachers will directly influence bargaining by demanding contract settlements that include "career" steps, longevity schedules, or annual bonuses. If teacher unions do in fact bargain for those who are employed at the time of settlement, future agreements will reflect the concerns and demands of those teachers in the majority—the senior teachers. The concern of the senior teachers will center on providing more dollars at the maximum of the salary schedule.

The Mediator and Teacher: School-Board
Collective Bargaining

The conclusions and statements of Doherty reflect an understanding and appreciation for collective bargaining generally and teacher–school-board collective bargaining specifically. However, his suggestions concerning the role of the neutral, and particularly the role of the mediator, in teacher–school-board collective bargaining is bitterly disappointing. To be considered a "settlement freak," or "mealy-mouthed," or only capable of judging a continuing impasse as a "loathsome social disease" is unacceptable. To Doherty's suggestion that

> Even in those circumstances where school boards and administrators are eager to "take the union on" on this issue, it is not likely they will succeed. In nearly all instances the issue would go to impasse, and a mediator or a fact finder would be brought in to help resolve the issue. In most instances these neutrals become the ally of the union since most of them, to use the pejorative, are "settlement freaks."

and his conclusion that

> If neutrals are involved in the bargaining, then one can almost be assured that the employer will make concessions because there can be no end to the impasse unless concessions are forthcoming, and neutrals regard a continuing impasse as they would a particularly loathsome social disease.

my response is, "Bob, you could not be more wrong." The fact finders and interest arbitrators need not be defended in this response for they are fully capable of justifying or rationalizing their role in the collective-bargaining process, but to conclude that the full-time mediator is not a professional who is depended on by both parties to resolve their bargaining differences is erroneous.

It is not necessary to discuss or analyze the differences between mediation, fact finding, and arbitration. It is necessary, however, to clarify what a mediator is and what biases mediators have. Mediation is a continuation of the process of face-to-face collective bargaining by the representatives of labor and management. It is not and should not be considered as a substitute for the process of bargaining. The mediator has a responsibility *to* and works *with* both parties to the process. To suggest that the mediator becomes an ally of either party is wrong; the mediator is an ally to the process of collective bargaining, not an ally to either party. The parties to teacher–school-board collective bargaining must recognize the biases and expectations that mediators have. I contend that successful mediators reflect the following biases:

1. Collective bargaining is a reasonable system to determine the terms and conditions of employment.
2. The settlement of a collective-bargaining dispute is an end in and of itself.
3. There is no impasse that cannot be settled by the parties.
4. Collective bargaining is a voluntary process and is therefore best settled by the parties themselves.
5. The process of collective bargaining is not a simple, pleasant, or necessarily satisfying experience, but it results in a settlement mutually agreed on by the parties.

I would not deny that mediators are settlement-prone; it is an admitted bias. Doherty's conclusion, however, suggests that the mediator becomes used to influencing the outcome of collective bargaining. Such a conclusion is wrong. The mediator's role is to provide the parties the means to reach a settlement, not to influence its outcome.

Concluding Thoughts on Education and
Collective Bargaining

Doherty's article raises important questions concerning the influence of collective bargaining on education and particularly student achievement. In many cases the impact of collective bargaining in education is predictable based on private-sector and other public-sector bargaining experiences. In other cases the impact is unique to education. An evaluation of collective bargaining and education does provide some significant conclusions.

Outcome of Collective Bargaining

Collective bargaining in education has

1. resulted in a "sameness" of terms and conditions of employment
2. reduced class size and the amount of teacher-student contract time

3. established salary schedules that reflect the interests of the majority of teachers employed at the time of settlement
4. improved the general economic interests of all teachers as opposed to the economic good of individual teachers
5. provided, through the grievance procedure, a system of workplace democracy not traditionally found in a non-collective-bargaining environment.

Process of Bargaining

Doherty suggests that collective bargaining is a boiling pot of "concessions," "pressures," and "neutrals" which is reserved only for management. I disagree wholeheartedly. Yes, the process of bargaining does take place in a concession environment, but the environment involves both labor and management. The desire for "things one does not have" or "things that one wants to get rid of" is found with both parties. The making of a concession is a dimension of the process that both parties must deal with if an agreement is to be reached. The pressure to reach an agreement—in reality, the pressure of not reaching an agreement—must be faced and evaluated by both parties, not management alone or labor alone. Certainly, the extent and intensity of the pressure will vary from day to day, bargaining session to bargaining session, or with the changing economic and community pressures. The environment, however, is one in which both parties must operate.

The role of the mediator within this system is to seek settlement. In the search for settlement, a recognition of and the use of pressure is inherent. The use of pressure by mediators needs no apology. But the pressure found in the bargaining environment influences both parties. If it is the object of the parties to reach a settlement, the mediator must be used to develop alternatives that are acceptable to the parties. The decision, however, to accept alternatives, make concessions, or reach an agreement always rests with the parties themselves. It is their decision. It is not the decision of the mediator. To the mediator there is no such thing as a "bad" settlement; all settlements are "good" because they are reached by the parties. As Tom McCarthy, Staff Mediator of the California State and Conciliation Service has concluded, "if that be amoral then let it be amoral."[4] The role of the mediator is to work within the unique environment of each bargaining relationship in an attempt to find that "package" that can be agreed to by the parties, not to use the system or the environment to effect the outcome of the negotiations for the particular advantage of labor or management.

Role of the Work Stoppage

If there are true concerns regarding the concessions being made by management in the bargaining process, because of the pressures, the concession environment, fact finder or arbitrators' decisions, or settlement-freak mediators, which adversely affect student achievement, then it is imperative that a system of impasse resolution be developed allowing for the parties to resist completely the loss or concession of a major issue. Where there are issues that labor or management consider so important, each should have the opportunity to make the issue a test of strength. If one is concerned that a subject of bargaining, which has a substantial impact on student achievement, will be "given away" in the environment of bargaining or lost through an arbitrator's decision, then it seems logical to conclude that there are issues over which the parties should have the right to strike or lockout. There are things that are worse than a strike or lockout.

Stability of Bargaining

The effectiveness of the bargaining process in education is unstable because of the high turnover of negotiating-committee members of both school boards and teacher unions. As a mediator, this instability concerns me. In many cases, it appears that those on negotiating committees view the experience as literally "doing time." Following the "pennance" of serving on a negotiating committee, too many considered it thereafter someone else's responsibility. One of the lessons labor and management in the education sector must learn is the necessity for some continuity in bargaining leadership positions. The increasing role of the full-time labor and management professionals will cure to some extent this somewhat disabling bargaining phenomena.

Importance of the Personnel Function

Collective bargaining has dramatically identified for management the importance of the personnel function within the organization. Labor cost for a school board is overwhelming in relation to total cost. It is probably the most labor-intensive industry found in our society. Collective bargaining has demanded a recognition by management and policymakers of the importance of the personnel function. If nothing else, collective bargaining in education and public employment generally, has solved any unemployment problem for industrial-relations graduates.

Identification of Management

The bargaining process has forced the identification of those who are management—whether "educational leaders" want to be or not. Doherty's earlier identification of the one characteristic—effective building supervision and management—having as much influence on student achievement as any other emphasizes this outcome. The process has put in clear perspective that there are those who are paid to manage and there are those who are paid to teach. Principals and assistant principals still may be "educational leaders," but they must also manage buildings, supplies, equipment, and expensive manpower. They must ultimately be judged on how well they manage these resources in producing the desired educational outcomes.

Notes

1. John Heim and Lewis Perl. *The Educational Production Function: Implications for Educational Manpower Policy.* Ithaca, New York: Institute of Public Employment, New York State School of Industrial and Labor Relations, Cornell University, June 1974.

2. Hopefully I have included the professions of all those responding to Doherty's article as well as that of the author.

3. Doherty does conclude that there is a strong relationship between the amount of student-teacher contact and student achievement.

4. Tom McCarthy, Mediator, California State Conciliation Service. Remarks made at the 1980 NPELRA Convention, March 5, 1980.

10 Epilogue

George W. Angell

The purpose of this section is not to analyze, compare, or evaluate statements made by the various contributors. Each statement was prepared independently and is left to stand on its own merit. Rather, this section is an attempt to provide some afterthoughts that may help to bring the two lead essays and the commentaries into common perspective without rehashing the points already elaborated.

Interestingly, Doherty and I each attempted to be cautious about arriving at hard and fast conclusions. We were too cautious in the eyes of those who agreed with our tentative conclusions and not cautious enough for those who disagreed. Fair enough! We used a widely different approach to the analysis of the current scenes in teacher bargaining, probably because the studies of higher and lower education and the data available are so different in character and quality. Basic objectives of lower education are usually stated in terms more tangible and measurable than are those in higher education. Thousands of relatively scientific studies of student achievement in lower education have been evolving in increasingly sophisticated format over the past century. No comparable effort has been attempted for higher education. Yet, each of us in his own way was critical of unions, management, neutrals, and others who have been on the frontiers of public-sector bargaining during the sixties and seventies. In retrospect, I believe we failed to give them sufficient credit for plowing new ground, overcoming incredible obstacles, and building a firm foundation for future progress. Perhaps most significantly, each of us, for different reasons, highlighted the political aspects of bargaining especially as we expect it to develop in the future.

Our most serious criticism of teacher bargaining, expressed in different terms, was related to the fact that bargaining inherently is directed toward the attainment of narrow self-interests often at the possible expense of educational quality. Doherty suggested that public pressures may cause legislatures to establish certain elements of "discipline" that he now finds lacking in public-sector bargaining. In turn, I suggested that each party needs to reform itself before public pressures force change. The current national mood of conservatism as expressed in the 1980 elections will certainly encourage self-examination and possibly reform earlier than I could anticipate when preparing the original manuscript months before the election.

In respect to these suggested reforms, I was impressed by the fact that several commentators appealed for understanding of teacher bargaining as a "sub-system" of American society and suggested that each party (union, management, neutral) to the subsystem be judged in terms of its special mission (rather than in terms of the common good) and that the bargaining process itself be appraised within the broader context of the total American eco-political system. This is a telling argument. One union or one group of unions surely cannot be fairly viewed in isolation from all the other unions and special-interest lobbies that shape the American way of life. Of course each union pursues narrow self-interests. That is its legal, inherent function and it must be analyzed in terms of function not social philosophy. Those of us who wish to philosophize about bargaining should pose a larger question: "Is teacher bargaining functioning well as a part of the total lobby-bargaining action that determines policy at the national, state and local levels?" And ultimately we should ask whether or not lobbies and bargaining offer the best means of expressing the democratic philosophy as stated in the Constitution of the United States. Doherty and I avoided these larger questions and wisely so, I believe.

Somewhere, somehow, I have come to feel that any group of educated people should and could find a reasonable way to set aside narrow interests when larger interests of the common good were in jeopardy. And this feeling has been reinforced by the fact that I have observed some faculty unions and university executives who, on a regular basis, have foregone personal gain in the interest of broader social purpose. I also have faith that, as in the past, these microcosms of social excellence will become the examples from which total society will eventually benefit most.

Index

About the Contributors

Woodley B. Osborne, a graduate of Trinity College and New York University School of Law, is currently in private law practice in Washington, D.C., with the law firm of Nassau and Osborne. He served as the first director of collective bargaining for the American Association of University Professors and prior to that was counsel to the Air Line Pilots Association.

Anthony V. Sinicropi is John F. Murray Professor of Industrial Relations at the University of Iowa, chairman of the Department of Industrial Relations and Human Resources, and director of the Industrial Relations Institute. Professor Sinicropi has served as a consultant for several government organizations, including the Social Security Administration; he is a member of the Board of Directors of the National Academy of Arbitrators and is president of the Society of Professionals in Dispute Resolution. Among his recent publications is *Iowa Labor Laws.*

Robert D. Helsby is the director of a Carnegie Foundation–supported project to aid public-employment labor-relations boards and commissions throughout the country to increase their efficiency and competency. When the New York State Public Employees' Fair Employment Act (Taylor law) was passed by the legislature in 1967, Dr. Helsby was appointed as the first chairman of the New York State Public Employment Relations Board and held that position for ten years. In 1971–1972 Dr. Helsby served as president of the Association of Labor Mediations, and in 1973-1974 he became the first president of the Society of Professionals in Dispute Resolution.

David Kuechle is professor of labor relations at the Harvard University Graduate School of Education and educational chairman of Harvard University's Institute for Educational Management. Mr. Kuechle received the J.D. degree from the University of Wisconsin in 1954 and subsequently received the master's degree and doctorate from Harvard University. He worked for seven years as industrial-relations supervisor for the A.O. Smith Corporation in Milwaukee before embarking on a teaching career. Mr. Kuechle is an active arbitrator, mediator, and labor-relations consultant.

Robert E. Doherty is associate dean for academic affairs at the New York State School of Industrial and Labor Relations, Cornell University. Mr. Doherty is a mediator, fact-finder, and arbitrator in public-sector disputes and has published widely on problems of bargaining in public education.

John E. Dunlop is currently manager of negotiations for the National Education Association (NEA). He has been employed by the NEA since 1968, serving during this period as a field representative, a negotiations specialist, a chief negotiator for the Hawaii State Teachers Association, and the assistant director for negotiations planning. He has published articles in *Journal of Law and Education, Cornell University,* and *NEA Bargaining Quarterly.*

R. Theodore Clark, Jr., is a partner with the firm of Seyfarth, Shaw, Fairweather and Geraldson, Chicago, where he represents both private- and public-sector clients with respect to a wide variety of labor-law problems. He is an instructor in public-sector labor-relations law at Northwestern University Law School and has served as a consultant to the Committee on Economic Development (CED) for its study on labor relations in state and local government. Mr. Clark is co-author of *Labor Relations in the Public Sector: Cases and Materials.*

Peter E. Obermeyer is director of the Minnesota Bureau of Mediation Services. He has been a partner of Labor Relations Associates, Inc., where he represented public employers in all phases of labor relations, a negotiator for the State of Minnesota, and the chapter manager of the National Electrical Contractor's Association. From 1972 to 1979, he served as vice-chairman and chairman of the Public Employment Relations Board.

About the Editor

George W. Angell has been a college teacher, department chairman, dean, and college president. Upon his retirement after twenty years as president of the State University of New York College of Arts and Science at Plattsburgh, he was director of the Academic Collective Bargaining Information Service in Washington, D.C., until 1977. He is the editor and chief author for *Handbook of Faculty Bargaining,* and he has published many articles and monographs on the subject of faculty bargaining.